CAN SALVATION GET YOU INTO HEAVEN?

THE ANSWER IS...

Yes!

PATRICIA S. TANNER

IBG Publications, Inc.

PATRICIA S. TANNER

IBG
PUBLICATIONS
Putting the POWER in your pen!

Published by I.B.G. Publications, Inc., a Power to Wealth Company

Web address: www.ibgpublications.com

admin@ibgpublications.com / 904-419-9810

Copyright, 2024 by Patricia S. Tanner

IBG Publications, Inc., Orange Park, FL

ISBN: 978-1-956266-81-8

Tanner, Patricia S.
Can Salvation Get You Into Heaven? The Answer Is Yes!

Printed in the United States of America.

Dedication

This book is dedicated to the special people in my life who I love most. Please share in my words of admiration, love, respect and honor for those who God has entrusted me with.

Dear TJ,

At just 21 years old, you've already shown incredible courage and strength, stepping up as a leader in our family. It fills my heart with pride to see you embrace the values and lessons I've always tried to teach you. You are so intelligent, resourceful, and determined, and I'm constantly amazed by the man you are becoming.

God chose me, out of all people, to be your mother, and for that, I am deeply grateful. It's an honor to guide you, love you, and watch you grow. Always remember to carry yourself with patience and humility.

The Bible reminds us in **Proverbs 16:32**, *"Better a patient person than a warrior, one with self-control than one who takes a city."* Being slow to anger will serve you well, my little TJ.

Continue to listen to God's voice in all you do. Let His wisdom guide your choices, especially when it comes to finances and making wise decisions. As **Proverbs 21:20** teaches us, *"The wise store up choice food and olive oil, but fools gulp theirs down."* Save wisely and think ahead; this will set you up for a stable and prosperous future.

TJ, I am beyond proud to be your mother. Keep leading with love, wisdom, and faith. Always trust that God has a purpose for your life and walk boldly in that truth. I love you.

Dear Kelvin,

I could not be prouder of you for having the courage to join the Army. It was a wise decision, one that shaped you into the incredible man you are today—strong, handsome, intelligent, independent, and hardworking. Your journey is a testament to your resilience and determination.

As you continue this path, remember to never allow PTSD or any mental battles to take control of your life. If you conquer your mind, you can conquer anything.

The Bible reminds us in **2 Corinthians 10:5** to *"Take captive every thought to make it obedient to Christ."* When your mind is racing, pray. Seek God's peace, which surpasses all understanding. I know you weren't raised in the church, but you were raised by my mom, who embodied the very essence of love. God is love, and in many ways, Mom reflected His character.

If you have love, Kelvin, you have everything you need to build an amazing life, because love overcomes all evil. Keep God first in everything you do, and let love guide your actions.

Kelvin, you were my firstborn, and it was through you that I found the strength to create a better life for us when I was just 17. God gave me the privilege of raising you, well mom raised you, but I lived in the house LOL, and I'm so grateful to be your mom. You are the rock of this family, the one who keeps us united. That's a role you've taken on with grace and strength.

Over the past three years, I've grown closer to God in ways I never imagined. I can't live without Him, and I want that same relationship for you. Keep your heart open to Him, Kelvin. Remember what your granddaddy taught you—save your money and spend wisely.

Life is full of battles, but with God on your side and love in your heart, you'll always come out victorious. I love you.

Dear Shay,

Watching you blossom from a cocoon into a beautiful butterfly has been one of the greatest joys of my life. I love you more deeply than words could ever express. I know you may not feel that love fully in your heart because of the mental wounds inflicted by someone close to us. Whether you acknowledge it or not, that pain is a stronghold that needs to be broken. Only then will you see life for what it truly is—a gift, full of beauty and grace.

Stay connected with your brothers and sisters, no matter how upset or distant you may feel at times. You are the bridge for them, the one who can guide them to know Jesus and His love. Never underestimate the power of your role in their lives.

I'll never forget when you were little, and you passed away in my arms. In that moment, I refused to let go; I prayed, and God gave you back to me. Just as I prayed for Him to save you, He answered your prayers when you asked for Gucci and blessed you with Owen. He is always listening, Shay.

You often ask, "Mom, what will I do if you're not here?" My answer will always be the same: *LIVE*. You know Jesus, and He is your anchor. Open your heart fully to Him and stop wavering in your faith. On the other side of this life is heaven, and in heaven, there is eternal peace. That's the promise of God's love, and it's what this journey is all about.

Never stop praying, Shay. Remember that we'll see each other again, but until then, stay the course. Let Psalm 23, your favorite passage, be your comfort before you sleep: *"The Lord is my shepherd; I shall not want..."*

I want you to know that I never took to heart the hurtful things you've said to me. I knew it wasn't you—it was the enemy trying to use you against me as I stepped into my higher purpose. Through it all, I've never held hatred in my heart. My love for you remains unwavering, even in the face of anger or misunderstanding.

Finally, stop shopping so much and start saving, just like your granddaddy always taught you. Remember what the Bible says about true beauty in **1 Peter 3:3-4**: *"Your beauty should not come from outward adornment, such as elaborate hairstyles and the wearing of gold jewelry or fine clothes. Rather, it should be that of your inner self, the unfading beauty of a gentle and quiet spirit, which is of great worth in God's sight."*

You are a light, Shay, and I'm so grateful to be your mom. Keep shining, and never forget how much you are loved. Your decision is always the right decision, so make it and trust God. I love you.

Dear Eona,

I am so proud of you for living the American dream. Among all my natural children, you are the only one to build your own family, and it fills my heart with joy. You are the glue that holds everything together.

Keep nurturing that bond, ensuring that your family and your siblings grow stronger with each passing year. Make it a priority to bring your siblings together for holidays, birthdays, and fun vacations. Those moments will create memories that last a lifetime.

You are the creative side of me, and I'm not surprised by how you organize and plan everything so perfectly. You always have a system in place to keep things running smoothly, and I admire that about you.

Seeing you as a mother now makes me incredibly proud. You finally understand the sacrifices I made and the unconditional love I have for all my children. I know you joke about who my favorite is and let me just say—the answer will go with me to my grave! (LOL)

Thank you, Eona, for letting me chastise you in front of your siblings. You knew it was all love, and because of your example, they knew how to straighten up quickly. Look at you now—beautiful, athletic, smart, happy, funny, and full of love. God truly blessed me when He gave me you.

Hold tight to the values of marriage and family. In a world full of brokenness, you are proof that unity and love can prevail. Like I told Shay, make your decisions with confidence and trust God to guide you.

As it says in **Proverbs 3:5-6**, *"Trust in the Lord with all your heart and lean not on your own understanding; in all your ways submit to Him, and He will make your paths straight."*

And always remember, as **Hebrews 11:1** teaches us: *"Now faith is confidence in what we hope for and assurance about what we do not see."* Keep your faith strong, my little Eona. Trust God in every step you take. I love you more than words can express, Eona. Thank you for being everything I could ever hope for in a daughter.

Dear Tavica,

I am so proud and grateful that God allowed me to raise you as my own daughter. You've always been a blessing in my life, and I cherish every moment we've shared.

I know you've battled with self-esteem at times, but never forget that you are far more than what you see in the mirror. Open the Bible and let God remind you of your worth. He created you beautifully and with purpose.

One of the things I admire most about you is your independence and maturity. You've always needed very little guidance from me, which speaks volumes about your character and wisdom. I've watched you face struggles, find solutions, and achieve great things. You've proven time and again that you can do anything you set your mind to—even changing a flat tire! (LOL)

Stay close to the church and immerse yourself in God's Word. You were raised in the faith, and you know Jesus. Let Him guide your steps. Remember, as it says in **2 Corinthians 1:20**, *"For no matter how many promises God has made, they are 'Yes' in Christ. And so through Him, the 'Amen' is spoken by us to the glory of God."* Trust in His will and know that if something isn't working out, it's because He has a better plan for you.

Don't be too hard on yourself when it comes to relationships. You are a beautiful, intelligent, and strong woman. Yes, you're picky, but that's okay! Let God bring the right man into your life in His perfect timing.

Proverbs 3:5-6 reminds us: *"Trust in the Lord with all your heart and lean not on your own understanding; in all your ways submit to Him, and He will make your paths straight."*

Tavica, I love you deeply, and as you always remind me—you are my daughter, not my stepdaughter. I wouldn't have it any other way. You are a shining light in my life, and I'm so proud of the woman you've become.

Dear Alexis,

From the moment you came into my life, I've been grateful every single day to have you as my baby girl. I'm so proud of you for building a beautiful family of your own. Your two precious children need you, and I know you'll raise them with love and strength, just as you were raised.

I see the hurt and pain in your eyes sometimes, and it breaks my heart. But Alexis, when those moments come, I want you to fall to your knees and cry out to God. He is your comforter and your refuge.

As the Bible says in **2 Corinthians 1:3-4**, *"Praise be to the God and Father of our Lord Jesus Christ, the Father of compassion and the God of all comfort, who comforts us in all our troubles."* Trust Him to carry your burdens and bring peace to your soul.

You've always been brilliant—a straight-A student in school and an honor roll achiever in college. That didn't surprise me a bit! Your determination and intelligence have always been evident.

Now, as you raise your children, instill in them the same love for God that you were taught. Remember **Proverbs 22:6**, *"Train up a child in the way he should go: and when he is old, he will not depart from it."*

And about those braces you've always wanted—don't worry, your time will come! (LOL)

But when you look in the mirror now, what do you see? I'll tell you what I see: a virtuous woman, full of grace and strength. **Proverbs 31:10** describes you perfectly: *"Who can find a virtuous woman? For her price is far above rubies."* That's you, Alexis.

Thank you for your service in the medical field, whether it's in a doctor's office or hospital. It's a calling that suits you perfectly. I can see you growing and thriving in this profession, making a difference in the lives of others.

Like Tavica, you've always been independent, needing little from me. That shows your maturity and strength. But more than anything, I know that God has you, and that's enough for my heart to rest easy. I love you, Alexis, and one day, I'll see you on the other side. Until then, keep trusting in God and walking in His light.

Dear June and Sam,

We are all we've got. No matter what life throws at us, we'll always have each other. As the years go by, let's stay close, not just for ourselves but for our children too. They'll need the strength of family, and we must be there for them, just as we've been for one another.

Please, always look out for my kids, just as I'd do for you. Take care of Mom's house and those dogs—yes, even the dogs! (LOL)

Keep your heads up, because one day we'll all be reunited with Mom and Dad. On that day, there will be no more struggles, pain, sadness, loneliness, brokenness, or heartache—only God's love and peace. It's time for us to get back to church. June don't put off getting baptized. Don't wait until the last minute, it's time to make that commitment now.

Sam, I want you to know I forgive you for chopping off my dolls' heads when we were kids (LOL). We've come a long way since then, and my love for you has only grown. I'm praying that we all get caught up together in the rapture, ready to meet God in eternal joy. Let's make sure we're prepared!!

Philippians 4:6-7 reminds us, *"Do not be anxious about anything, but in every situation, by prayer and petition, with thanksgiving, present your requests to God. And the peace of God, which transcends all understanding, will guard your hearts and your minds in Christ Jesus."*

I love you both so much. No matter what happens, know that I'm always praying for us. Let's stay strong together and keep our eyes on God.

Dear Gail,

For over 36 years, you've been more than just a friend, you've been my anchor through life's storms. You've stood by my side as I raised my children, offering wisdom and love every step of the way. You were there when I faced the heartbreak of losing my parents, grieving with me as if they were your own. You've seen me through the ups and downs of relationships, the joys and heartbreaks, and even the rollercoaster of family arguments.

Through it all, you've been my coach, my counselor, and my constant source of comfort. You have this incredible ability to ease my mind and soothe my pain, always knowing the right words to say or simply when to just be there in silence. But perhaps the greatest gift you've given me is keeping me close to God.

You've reminded me time and again of His love and faithfulness, guiding me back to prayer and faith when I've felt lost. Your encouragement and spiritual strength have been a light in my darkest moments.

Gail, you've been there through every chapter of my life—through the joy, heartache, and everything in between—and I can't thank you enough for the love and guidance you've given me.

As the Bible says in **Joshua 1:9**, *"Be strong and courageous. Do not be afraid; do not be discouraged, for the Lord your God will be with you wherever you go."* You've shown me the power of courage and faith, and for that, I am forever grateful. I love you more than words can express.

Dear Terrell,

I don't even know where to start but let me first say how incredibly thankful I am to have you in my life. You've been my guide in so many ways—from helping me navigate through life's challenges to literally guiding me when I got lost in Sanford (LOL) and even on the highway!

Your common sense and level-headedness have been a lifesaver more times than I can count. You've been my rock during some of my toughest moments, especially when I was struggling with my faith. You helped me find my way back to God, and for that, I'll always be grateful. That's what real men do—they care about your eternal life because that's what truly matters.

This life is temporary, but nothing compares to a man who leads you to grow in your relationship with God. Thank you for being that man. I'm so proud of the incredible father you are, raising your children with love and dedication as both mom and dad. Whether it's cooking meals, driving to school, celebrating graduations, or throwing kid parties, you handle it all with such grace. Trust me, as someone who raised six, I feel your pain (LOL). But you do it with a strength and commitment that's truly inspiring. Oh, and don't forget—keep that toilet seat down (LOL)!

You've become the man your mother always dreamed of—strong, smart, charismatic, and full of love for God and your family. I admire your dedication to your friends and your unwavering faith. Keep up the amazing work, stay focused, and keep growing in God's grace. And of course, keep making that money, honey! (LOL)

I'm so proud of you, Terrell, and I'm grateful every day to have you in my life. As the Bible says in **Proverbs 24:5**, *"The wise man is strong, yea, a man of knowledge increaseth strength."*

You're strong as an ox, Terrell—strong in body, in spirit, and in your faith. Keep pressing forward with the strength God has given you. ***Love always, Patricia!!***

TABLE OF CONTENTS

PATRICIA S. TANNER

Chapter 1

Who Is God?

And God said unto Moses, I Am That I Am: and he said, thus shalt thou say unto the children of Israel, I Am hath sent me unto you.

~Exodus 3:14 (KJV)

Genesis 1:1 says, *"In the beginning God created the heavens and the earth.*

STOP!

After reading this first sentence, it's not rocket science to look up in the sky to see the heavens then look at the ground to see the foundation you stand on is called Earth. Let me explain. If you read **Genesis chapters 1 and 2**, you will gain a full understanding of who God is, not what He did; but who He is.

I want you to take a moment to pause and read these passages of scriptures before you proceed further to gain a better understanding of the message. I don't want to spoil your reading, because after I read it, the words came alive for me, as I know it will be the same for you. Therefore, I want you to receive the same experience I received when I read it.

I know it's hard for you to believe, so let me put it like this. The Bible was written by the Holy Spirit, not man. Man was the vessel used by God to bring the writing from the spiritual realm into the natural realm; but man did not write the Bible. It is impossible to experience what is spiritual without the element of the natural, when you *live* in the natural world.

I know that's deep but walk with me. I'll talk about that more in detail in another chapter. But for now, let's find out who God is.

God is the creator of all things. He is powerful, holy, life, truth, light, love, and all-knowing to name a few of His attributes. *All* these things are God.

Throughout Genesis, God told you who He was. He said it, and it was….that is God. Anything that is life, is God. He's not a thing, He *is* the thing.

For example, if God said, let there be light, then God is light. While He is light, He's everywhere at the same time, just as light is and exposes everything in its path. You can run but you can't hide from God or His light.

God is omniscient, He knows everything, all the time. Go outside and look around. What do you see? Let me give you the answer you seek. You see GOD.

Many ask, "How do you know that?"

I know these things because I know God.

The Nature & Characteristics Of God

Understanding the nature and characteristics of God is foundational to discerning His role in salvation and our relationship with Him. The Bible provides thorough insights into His attributes, which reveal His nature as both supernatural and personal.

When Moses encountered God in the burning bush, he asked for God's name to assure the Israelites of His authority. God replied:

"I am that I am. This is what you are to say to the Israelites: 'I AM has sent me to you'" (**Exodus 3:14, NIV**).

This declaration encapsulates God's eternal, self-sustaining, and unchanging nature. Unlike created beings, God exists independently of time, space, or human comprehension. He simply *is*. The phrase, 'I am that I am' signifies:

1. <u>**Eternal Existence**</u>: God is beyond beginning and end (**Psalm 90:2**).

2. <u>**Sovereignty**</u>: His authority and existence do not depend on external factors (**Revelation 1:8**).

3. <u>**Faithfulness**</u>: God's constancy assures us that His promises and character remain steadfast (**Malachi 3:6**).

Let's Go Deeper...

Before I describe God, lets analyze your situation. How well do you know yourself? When you look in the mirror, what do you see?

I will let you think about that one.

In the book of **Galatians 5:22**, the Bible describes who God is. According to the fruit of His Spirit, He is love, joy, peace, patience, kindness, goodness, faithfulness, gentleness, and self-control. God is sinless, and most importantly, God is Spirit. He is eternal, He doesn't die, He's without form, He doesn't age, and He's omnipresent, meaning He can be anywhere at any time.

But the fruit of the Spirit is love, joy, peace, forbearance, kindness, goodness, faithfulness, gentleness and self-control. Against such things there is no law.
~**Galatians 5:22-23**

Here are 10 points that you need to understand about who God is. Some points I have briefly shared, but now I will provide the scriptures to validate the claims of who God is. I will elaborate on them briefly to give you more clarity on His essence and nature.

1. God Is Eternal

God has no beginning or end. He exists outside the constraints of time and space.

- *"Before the mountains were born or you brought forth the whole world, from everlasting to everlasting you are God"* (**Psalm 90:2**).

- *"I am the Alpha and the Omega," says the Lord God, "who is, and who was, and who is to come, the Almighty"* (**Revelation 1:8**).

2. God Is Omnipotent (All-Powerful)

God has unlimited power to accomplish His purposes.

- *"Ah, Sovereign Lord, you have made the heavens and the earth by your great power and outstretched arm. Nothing is too hard for you"* (**Jeremiah 32:17**) .

- *"Our God is in heaven; he does whatever pleases him"* (**Psalm 115:3**).

---

3. God Is Omniscient (All-Knowing)

God knows everything—past, present, and future—including our thoughts and intentions.

- *"Great is our Lord and mighty in power; his understanding has no limit"* (**Psalm 147:5**).

- *"Nothing in all creation is hidden from God's sight. Everything is uncovered and laid bare before the eyes of Him to whom we must give account"* (**Hebrews 4:13**).

---

4. God Is Omnipresent

God is always present everywhere, sustaining all of creation.

- *"Where can I go from your Spirit? Where can I flee from your presence? If I go up to the heavens, you are there; if I make my bed in the depths, you are there"* (**Psalm 139:7-8**).

- *"Am I only a God nearby," declares the Lord, "and not a God far away?"* (**Jeremiah 23:23**)

---

5. God Is Holy

God is utterly pure, righteous, and separated from sin.

- *"Holy, holy, holy is the Lord Almighty; the whole earth is full of his glory"* (**Isaiah 6:3**).

- *"But just as he who called you is holy, so be holy in all you do; for it is written: 'Be holy, because I am holy'"* (**1 Peter 1:15-16**).

---

6. God Is Love

God's nature is defined by perfect love, which He demonstrated through Jesus Christ.

- *"Whoever does not love does not know God, because God is love"* (**1 John 4:8**).

- *"For God so loved the world that he gave his one and only Son, that whoever believes in him shall not perish but have eternal life"* (**John 3:16**).

---

7. God Is Just

God upholds righteousness and fairness. His judgments are true and impartial.

- *"For the Lord is righteous, he loves justice; the upright will see his face"* (**Psalm 11:7**).

- *"He will judge the world in righteousness; he will govern the peoples with justice"* (**Psalm 9:8**).

---

8. God Is Immutable (Unchanging)

God's nature, purposes, and promises never change.

- *"I the Lord do not change. So, you, the descendants of Jacob, are not destroyed"* (**Malachi 3:6**).

- *"Jesus Christ is the same yesterday and today and forever"* (**Hebrews 13:8**).

9. God Is Faithful

God always keeps His promises and remains true to His Word.

- *"The Lord is trustworthy in all He promises and faithful in all He does"* (**Psalm 145:13**).

- *"If we are faithless, He remains faithful, for He cannot disown Himself"* (**2 Timothy 2:13**).

10. God Is Sovereign

God reigns supreme over all creation and directs everything according to His will.

- *"The Lord has established His throne in heaven, and His kingdom rules over all"* (**Psalm 103:19**).

- *"And we know that in all things God works for the good of those who love Him, who have been called according to His purpose"* (**Romans 8:28**).

Each of these characteristics reveals God's majesty and draws us into deeper reverence and trust. His holiness demands our worship, His love invites our relationship, and His justice ensures that evil will not prevail. These attributes work in harmony, ensuring that God is both the righteous Judge and the loving Savior.

You Are The Image Of God

Let me ask you a question: Have you ever attended a funeral? I have and that's why I can tell the truth. When attending a funeral, I received an order of service. On the program, there was a time when it stated that friends and family can speak for two minutes. Now we know what type of church held these services, LOL!

As the program moved along, each person walked up and talked about how funny the person was, how loving the person was, how giving the person was, how friendly the person was, etc. You get it, right?

In other words, nobody mentioned how much money the person had, how many houses they owned, or their job description. NOPE! They described who that person was and how they lived their life. When you go to the graveyard, those same words are on the headstone. How you lived your life is a testament to who you were when you were alive here on earth.

Now remember, I said look inside the mirror and glance at who you see. Take one minute to describe yourself; this is how people see you. Looking at yourself leads me to the controversy about who God is. Is he *only* a Spirit? Well, the answer is NO! He is a three part being-Father, Son and Holy Spirit.

Go to the Bible and let's read **Genesis 1:26** which says, "*Then God said, let us make man, in our image to be like us.*" I know you're asking who "us" is, or "Who is God talking to?" That's too deep for you right now, so let's stay focused on God. We will go further into the 'why' of creating man in the next chapter.

The next verse **Genesis 1:27** says, "*So God created man in His own image. In the image of God, He created them; male and female He created them.*"

Guess what? **HE** DID IT!

Look at yourself *again* in the mirror.

Let's go to **Genesis 2:7**. It says, "*Then the Lord God formed the man from the dust of the ground. He breathed the breath of life into the man's nostrils, and the man became a living soul.*"

WOW. **Now**, man became a living soul.

> *And the very God of peace sanctify you wholly; and I pray God your whole spirit and soul and body be preserved blameless unto the coming of our Lord Jesus Christ.*
>
> **~I Thessalonians 5:23**

To conclude, God is Spirit, Soul, and Body, and so are you. Now you get it, GOD is just like you! You have a spirit that lives in a body and has a soul; a three separate entity like the Father, Son and Holy Spirit.

To best know Him, you must know yourself. There is so much more to explore about God, but we have lots of ground to cover here, so let's keep moving….

PATRICIA S. TANNER

Chapter 2

Why Were We Created?

And the Lord God formed man of the dust of the ground and breathed into his nostrils the breath of life; and man became a living soul.

-Genesis 2:7 (KJV)

From the very beginning of Scripture, the creation of mankind stands out as a pinnacle of God's creative work. **Genesis 1:27** declares: *"So God created mankind in his own image, in the image of God he created them; male and female he created them."* This foundational truth invites us to explore a profound question: Why did an all-sufficient, eternal God choose to create humanity?

The answer lies in understanding God's character and His divine purposes. God did not create man out of need, for He lacks nothing. Instead, He created mankind as an expression of His love, creativity, and desire for relationship. Humanity was uniquely fashioned to reflect God's glory, to steward His creation, and to live in fellowship with Him.

This chapter delves into the heart of God's purpose for mankind, exploring key truths such as:

1. **To Reflect His Image:** Humanity was designed to mirror God's character and represent Him on Earth (**Genesis 1:26-27**).

2. **For Relationship:** God created mankind to enjoy an intimate, loving relationship with Him (**John 17:3**).

3. **To Glorify Him:** Our highest purpose is to worship and glorify God in all we do (**Isaiah 43:7**).

4. **To Fulfill His Mission:** God gave mankind the mandate to steward and care for the Earth (**Genesis 2:15**).

5. **To Exercise Dominion Over Earth:** God gave man the responsibility to steward and care for the Earth, reflecting His authority and creativity (**Genesis 1:28**).

Through these truths, we see that mankind's creation was not random or purposeless, but intentional, rooted in God's sovereign plan. As we examine the reasons behind our existence, we are invited to rediscover the significance of our identity, value, and purpose in the Creator's grand design.

When the heavens and the earth were complete, God needed someone to oversee the earth and to oversee His creation. Remember, in chapter one, I mentioned our creation started with a discussion to create man. Allow me to walk you through these passages of scripture more in depth.

The Bible says in **Genesis 1:26** *"Then God said, "Let us make man in our image, to be like us. They will reign over the fish in the sea, the birds in the sky, the livestock, all the wild animals on the earth, and the small animals that scurry along the ground."* This verse shares God's intention and His thought process for creating man.

Genesis 1:27 says, HE DID!

Chapter 2 of Genesis verse 7 states that man was given a body to rule over all the earth. It says, *"Then the Lord God formed the man* *from the dust of the ground. He breathed the breath of life into the man's nostrils, and the man became a living soul."*

In that same chapter, verse 8, it says, *"God planted a garden in the east, and there he placed the man He created."* Let's keep reading, Verse 15 which says, *"The Lord God placed the man in the Garden of Eden to tend to watch over it."*

I can't make this stuff up! All you have to do is read it for yourself.

I bet you have a Bible in your home. The book probably has been sitting in your China cabinet or on a table that no one sits at, or in your glove box in your car, or on the side of your bed. Perhaps it's in the bathroom and not once, did you try to pick it up and read it. I didn't up until one year ago, when I was hungry for the word.

Here is my story.

I didn't want to start out with my story because the message of this book is more important than me. However, if I tell you where I was and where I am now, then you will continue reading this book. If you're willing, God will change your heart to believe and receive Him.

Anyway, here is my 2-minute miracle: There were 4 words I never thought I would ever face. These 4 words turned my life upside down. First, let me tell you who I am. My name is Patricia S. Tanner, and I was born and raised in Sanford, FL. My mom is Thai, and my dad is African American.

At the age of 16, I was pregnant with my first child while in high school. Two years later, I was pregnant with another child when I was graduating from high school and another one when I was graduating from college.

My final child was born at the age of 23 from a previous marriage. All in all, I made six figures all my life and I was able to achieve two master's degrees. My church life started as a Baptist when I was in my 20's but I was a workaholic and didn't attend regularly. I had a relationship with God, and I always talked to Him every day in prayer, but I never read the Bible.

I lost my dad in December 2016 to cancer and five years later, my mom was diagnosed with COVID-19. After praying night and day, I lost my mom thirty days after her diagnosis in January of 2021.

These four words destroyed me because I decided to put my mom to sleep and I told her when she woke up, I'll be right there. Then His four words came alive, "THY WILL BE DONE!!"

I was shocked that she passed away. God didn't answer my prayer. I was mad at God for a year and tried to commit suicide almost a year to her death. My friend tried to talk me out of it, and I didn't want to hear anything he had to say.

Interestingly enough, God had plans for me and the Holy Spirit put me in a trance. I typed a message on my phone and 30 seconds later, The Holy Spirit gave me 30 days of grieving. I realized that God had never left me, and He was always with me. He said, *"Everyone will know who Patricia Tanner is."*

I dismissed that information because I only had one best friend, and I wasn't on social media. Today, I'm a real estate broker, author of six books, and the inventor of a real estate game board called *Get*

Real Estateblished. I own a property management company, a real estate company, a tax business, a court reporting business, and an investment company. I have a non-profit organization, and my partner and I build homes in Sanford and flip homes everywhere. So yes, I'm a female in construction.

An old friend from high school saw my success in the community and my story blew up. I was on TV, radio, podcasts, newspapers, magazines, and I am an award winner of one of 100 of the most successful women in the world which I received in London. I'm also a candidate to receive a presidential award in December for all my success in my community.

A year ago, my friend influenced me to purchase and read a Bible for a 5-year-old. He said I needed milk, and I wasn't ready for the meat. That Bible changed my life. It got me hungry for the word. And now I can't stop seeking the knowledge and wisdom of the word.

My Faith Continued To Grow

An atheist told me about a church in Lake Mary. On day one, I attended. On day two, I was serving on the 10:30 AM usher/greeter team. One week later, I was part of a life group. Then the following month, I was in a Foundations Biblical training class. Next, I got re-baptized and downloaded an app called 'bless every home' to pray for my neighbors, and now I'm a leader on the usher greeter team and a table leader at my church.

Then those 4 words turned into 2 words because he brought grieving to me, to get me through it. Those 2 words are my living testimony, and those words are, "I SAID. God said, 'I SAID,' I can do all things through Christ Jesus who strengthen me."

When I'm battling my thoughts, "God said, my thoughts are higher than your thoughts and my ways are bigger than yours." When I could not stop crying, God said, "I'm here. I will never leave you nor forsake you." With that being said, I am striving towards my healing journey.

Now, let's get back to the chapter…

God intended for the earth to belong to man. Not an Angel, not Satan, not a Spirit, but MAN. The scriptures tell us that we were just like God, a spirit; before He blew breath into man, then he became a living soul.

Think of it like this: A body was created for the spirit to dwell inside. Put that thought in the back of your mind for now. I will come back to that. There is an answer, backed by scriptures.

We were created on earth to have dominion over the earth. This is the truth. Your answer simply says, we were placed on earth by God to dominate the earth over all things including the animals and the creatures. Therefore, God added a body and a soul to do all these things on earth.

Side Note: When Adam was in the garden, Satan told Eve to eat the fruit. **Genesis 3:1** says, *"The serpent was the shrewdest of all the wild animals the Lord God had made. One day he asked the woman, "Did God really say you must not eat the fruit from any of the trees in the garden?"*

Eve told Satan that she could not eat the fruit because God said she will die. Do not take my word for it, here is the scripture. **Genesis 3:3** says, Eve said, *"God said, 'You must not eat it or even touch it; if you do, you will die."*

Satan told Eve; you will not die. **Genesis 3:4-5** says, *"You won't die!"* the serpent replied to the woman. *"God knows that your eyes will be opened as soon as you eat it, and you will be like God, knowing both good and evil."*

God in this context, used the word "die" meaning that you will have knowledge of good and bad things; in other words, you will know the difference between right and wrong. When she ate it, she did not die.

Genesis 3:7 says, *"At that moment their eyes were opened, and they suddenly felt shame at their nakedness. So, they sewed fig leaves together to cover themselves."*

Just as Satan said, she did not fall dead to the ground. Satan did not know why God said that. After much research, you will "die" meant you will die without God; sin is the absence of God's presence. To be absent from God's presence is when you are doing wrong, which is called a sin that results in death. Allow me to prove it to you.

Pay close attention to the following verses-God then kicks them out of Eden and sin is explained. **Genesis 4:6-7** says, *"Why are you so angry?" the Lord asked Cain. "Why do you look so dejected? You will be accepted if you do what is right. But if you refuse to do what is right, then watch out! Sin is crouching at the door, eager to control you. But you must subdue it and be its master."*

Get ready for a wild adventure and open your mind and heart to hear what the Spirit of the Lord is saying to you. This scripture introduces the word, 'sin' for all those who did not know it. Now you learned that every man was born into sin because of Adam's decisions.

Hold that thought.

Genesis 49:10 says, *"The scepter will not depart from Judah, nor the ruler's staff from his descendants, until the coming of the one to whom it belongs, the one whom all nations will honor."*

This verse appears in the blessings and prophecies that Jacob (also called Israel) pronounced over his twelve sons before his death. These blessings were both a reflection on the sons' past actions and a prophetic glimpse into their future and the destinies of the tribes that would emerge from them. Always keep in mind that children of Israel are God's chosen people, also the descendants of Abraham.

If you can recall, I expressed about 5 reasons that God created man. Let us look at point #5 which is the foremost reason for His creation: to have dominion over the Earth.

In exercising dominion, we receive and carry His heavenly inheritance into the Earth, enjoying its benefits and distributing it to others. This inheritance was given through the Abrahamic covenant, which I will briefly go over so you can gain the best clarity on how God expects us to exercise dominion over the Earth.

The Abrahamic Covenant

The Abrahamic Covenant is a foundational element in the Bible, marking a pivotal moment in God's relationship with humanity. This covenant, established between God and Abraham, encompasses promises of land, descendants, and blessings, and serves as a cornerstone for the faith traditions of Judaism, Christianity, and Islam.

> *In the same day the Lord made a covenant with Abram, saying, "Unto thy seed have I given this land, from the river of Egypt unto the great river, the river Euphrates."*
> *~Genisis 15:18*

Key Components of the Abrahamic Covenant:

1. **Promise of Land**: God pledged to give Abraham and his descendants the land of Canaan, often referred to as the Promised Land. This promise is articulated in **Genesis 12:1** and further detailed in **Genesis 15:18-21**, where God specifies the land's boundaries.

2. **Promise of Descendants**: Despite Abraham and his wife Sarah being advanced in age and childless at the time, God assured Abraham that he would become the father of a great nation, with descendants as numerous as the stars. This is highlighted in **Genesis 15:5**.

3. **Promise of Blessing and Redemption**: God declared that through Abraham's lineage, all the families of the earth would be blessed, indicating a plan for universal redemption. This aspect is emphasized in **Genesis 12:3**.

Nature of the Covenant:

The Abrahamic Covenant is characterized as an unconditional covenant, meaning its fulfillment rests solely on God's faithfulness and not on human actions. This is evident in the covenant ceremony described in **Genesis 15**, where God alone passes between the pieces of the sacrificed animals, symbolizing His sole responsibility in upholding the covenant.

Exploring the Abrahamic Covenant gives us a clear indication of the love of God and His faithfulness. To institute such a covenant that is void of man's responsibility to do something to achieve it speaks volumes about the sovereignty of God. I personally feel like the Abrahamic covenant was not necessary, but then it was because man had aborted God's original plan for dominion through sin and disobedience by way of Adam. But we have such a loving Father that He came back after man's failures and made a promise to give man dominion through this covenant.

Through this covenant, man was given land, descendants, blessings and redemption. With a covenant like this, it seems as if obedience to God would be simple and achievable, right? Wrong.

His Covenants: Relationship With His Creation

Once Adam sinned, it withdrew the Adamic Covenant because man's dominion had been lost through sin. This break in relationship was so detrimental to God that He repented for the creation of man, and it grieved His heart (**Genesis 6:6**).

While the Father was grieved at man, He never relinquished His desire to be close to His creation. In my opinion, the best attribute of God is His love, and desire for relationship with His creation. He instituted His love by establishing additional covenants to display His unconditional love.

Along with the Abrahamic covenant, God also gave five other covenants because of His ongoing attempts to redeem man, display His love and ensure man received His royal inheritance. Let's take a brief look at the other covenants and the promises made by God to redeem His people and distribute their inheritance.

Here is a look at the other covenants God made:

1. The Adamic Covenant (Covenant with Adam)

Scripture: **Genesis 1:26–30; Genesis 2:16–17; Genesis 3:15**
Type: Conditional and Unconditional

- **Content:** God created Adam and Eve, giving them dominion over creation and the command to be fruitful and multiply. However, He also gave a condition: they must not eat from the tree of the knowledge of good and evil. When they disobeyed, humanity fell into sin, and God pronounced consequences but also promised redemption (**Genesis 3:15**), known as the protoevangelium, the first mention of the Gospel.

- **Key Promise:** A Savior would come to crush the serpent's head, signaling the ultimate defeat of sin and Satan.

2. The Noahic Covenant (Covenant with Noah)

Scripture: **Genesis 8:20–22; Genesis 9:1–17**
Type: Unconditional

- **Content:** After the flood, God promised never to destroy the Earth by flood again. He established a covenant with Noah and all living creatures, symbolized by the rainbow.

- **Key Promise:** Preservation of life and the stability of the natural order (**Genesis 9:11**).

3. The Abrahamic Covenant (Covenant with Abraham)

Scripture: **Genesis 12:1–3; Genesis 15:1–21; Genesis 17:1–14**
Type: Unconditional

- **Content:** God promised Abraham that He would make him a great nation, bless him, give his descendants the land of Canaan, and that through his seed, all nations of the earth would be blessed.

- **Key Promise:** The promise of a Messiah, who would come through Abraham's lineage (**Galatians 3:16**).

4. The Mosaic Covenant (Covenant with Moses)

Scripture: **Exodus 19–24; Deuteronomy 28–30**
Type: Conditional

- **Content:** God gave the Law (including the Ten Commandments) to Israel through Moses. This covenant was conditional: blessings for obedience and curses for disobedience. It defined Israel's relationship with God and set them apart as His chosen people.

- **Key Promise:** If Israel obeyed God's laws, they would prosper and be His treasured possession (**Exodus 19:5–6**).

---

5. The Priestly Covenant (Covenant with the Levites)

Scripture: **Numbers 25:10–13; Malachi 2:4–5**
Type: Unconditional

- **Content:** God made a covenant with Phinehas and the priestly line of Levi, promising them a perpetual priesthood.

- **Key Promise:** A priestly role in mediating between God and His people. This foreshadowed the ultimate High Priest, Jesus Christ (**Hebrews 7:24–25**).

---

6. The Davidic Covenant (Covenant with David)

Scripture: **2 Samuel 7:12–16; 1 Chronicles 17:11–14; Psalm 89:3–4**
Type: Unconditional

- **Content:** God promised David that his lineage would endure forever and that one of his descendants would establish an eternal kingdom. This covenant pointed directly to Jesus Christ, the Messiah, as the ultimate fulfillment.

- **Key Promise:** An everlasting kingdom through David's line (**Luke 1:32–33**).

---

7. The New Covenant

Scripture: **Jeremiah 31:31–34; Ezekiel 36:26–27; Luke 22:20; Hebrews 8:6–13**
Type: Unconditional

- **Content:** God promised to make a new covenant with His people, writing His laws on their hearts rather than tablets of stone. This covenant was fulfilled in Jesus Christ, who instituted it through His death and resurrection.

- **Key Promise:** Forgiveness of sins, a personal relationship with God, and the indwelling of the Holy Spirit (**Hebrews 8:10–12**).

The covenants demonstrate God's faithfulness to His promises and His unfolding plan of salvation. Each covenant builds upon the previous one, culminating in Jesus Christ, who fulfills every covenant. Through the New Covenant, believers are brought into a personal relationship with God, enjoying the ultimate purpose of all the covenants: reconciliation and eternal life with Him.

As you can see, God has made several attempts to bring His people close to His heart. He longs for relationship and closeness with His children; this is the sole reason for creating man. As you have explored many aspects of the creation of man, it is my hope that you are clear on why you were created in the likeness of God like Adam.

In the next chapter, we will visit the 10 commandments and why God instituted the law. I already know, you think the 10 commandments are not relevant today, or that Jesus cancelled out the law when He died on the cross. No, He did not cancel out the law, He *fulfilled* the law, huge difference. We are still expected to keep the 10 commandments and even the Levitical laws.

I told you you were in for a wild ride... Here we go!

Chapter 3

The Laws:
Ten Commandments

Think not that I am come to destroy the law, or the prophets: I am not come to destroy, but to fulfil.

-Matthew 5:17 (KJV)

These are the 10 commandments adapted straight from the Bible, from **Exodus 20:3-17:**

1. *I am the Lord your God, who rescued you from the land of Egypt, the place of your slavery.*

2. *You must not have any other god but me. "You must not make for yourself an idol of any kind or an image of anything in the heavens or on the earth or in the sea. You must not bow down to them or worship them, for I, the Lord your God, am a jealous God who will not tolerate your affection for any other gods. I lay the sins of the parents upon their children; the entire family is affected—even children in the third and fourth generations of those who reject me. But I lavish unfailing love for a thousand generations on those who love me and obey my commands.*

3. *You must not misuse the name of the Lord your God. The Lord will not let you go unpunished if you misuse his name.*

4. *Remember to observe the Sabbath day by keeping it holy. You have six days each week for your ordinary work, but the seventh day is a Sabbath day of rest dedicated to the Lord your God. On that day no one in your household may do any work. This includes you, your sons and daughters, your male*

and female servants, your livestock, and any foreigners living among you. For in six days the Lord made the heavens, the earth, the sea, and everything in them; but on the seventh day he rested. That is why the Lord blessed the Sabbath day and set it apart as holy.

5. *Honor your father and mother. Then you will live a long, full life in the land the Lord your God is giving you.*

6. *You must not murder.*

7. *You must not commit adultery.*

8. *You must not steal.*

9. *You must not testify falsely against your neighbor.*

10. *You must not covet your neighbor's house. You must not covet your neighbor's wife, male or female servant, ox or donkey, or anything else that belongs to your neighbor.*

Exodus 20:18 says, *"When the people heard the thunder and the loud blast of the ram's horn, and when they saw the flashes of lightning and the smoke billowing from the mountain, they stood at a distance, trembling with fear.*

Exodus 20:20 says, *"Don't be afraid," Moses answered them, "for God has come in this way to test you, and so that your fear of him will keep you from sinning!"*

The Bible emphasizes the importance of the Ten Commandments and warns about consequences for disobedience throughout the Old and New Testaments. While these commandments were issued to Moses, we can still see the consequences of disobeying them on the Earth today. Have you considered the steep consequences in our justice system for murder? Or for stealing?

Yes, we must keep the 10 commandments. If the justice system of this world has consequences for breaking the law (in the form of the 10 commandments), how much more than God's expectations of the same? This is why I mentioned in the last chapter that Jesus did not cancel out the law.

Why The Ten Commandments?

Let me give you a little history behind these commandments. These were the laws that God gave the children of Israel in the desert. God wanted to sanctify His people as a covenant community so everyone around them would understand the level of holiness and righteous of this community. God wanted His people to set the example of a community that was equal, no judgment, no sin, no diseases, no anger, no violence, no jealousy; just a chosen community full of wealth, joy, peace, kindness, and everything they needed, just like He did for Adam and Eve.

Exodus 23:25-26 says, *"You must serve only the Lord your God. If you do, I will bless you with food and water, and I will protect you from illness. There will be no miscarriages or infertility in your land, and I will give you long, full lives."*

Poor God.

I can feel the stress when I am reading the Bible and the sorrow in His heart. Think of your family. Do you want to be judged for their actions? Do you want to be held responsible for *their* mishaps? Do you want someone to see your child acting in an oblivious manner and they are a spitting image of you? They look exactly like you, yet they are living a life contrary to what you taught them! Think of how

God felt. He wanted a chosen community to be just like Him, who *looked* like Him.

Well, if you read the Bible that didn't last long. All God wanted was to rule over them and for them to obey the laws of the land. After forty days of being in the desert, they rebelled against God, despite all the miracles that occurred. They kept complaining about returning to a culture of people who did not see them as equals. They wanted to go back to slavery because it was all they knew along with the food they missed so much.

Sound like someone you know?

God got so angry, He cursed the people for their disobedience, then 40 days turned into 40 years. They never made it to the promised land, and they all died in the desert, except for a few chosen people. God started over with a new generation who entered the promised land.

You know what bothered me so much when I was reading this? The unbelief of the people shocked me although they experienced one miracle after another. It started in Egypt. The Israelites saw what God did when Pharaoh disobeyed a command. The torture of the Egyptians was unbelievable, yet that was not enough for them.

I'm only telling you this so you can read it yourself. You need to feel the experience as if you were standing there watching it. I could literally see myself standing in the city nearby with the Israelites watching the HELL that occurred when God protected his people...

Imagine you and your friend standing on the sidewalk waiting to cross the road and hail falls from the sky. You and him or her are side by side. The hail is hitting your friend, and you are not affected. Next, a disease breaks out all over the skin of your friend. You look around and everyone has the same skin disease except you. This is what occurred Egypt.

Now let's go to the desert.

These people did not have any food to eat. Moses prayed to God and food fell from the sky, water poured out from the earth, shelter followed them with a cloud both day and fire by night. All of this and they still did not believe it. Fast forward, Moses dies, Joshua, his assistant was the next leader in charge.

In **Exodus 32:33** God says, "*Whoever has sinned against me, I will blot out of my book*," in the context of idolatry, which breaks the first and second commandments. **Leviticus 26:14-46** outlines punishments for disobedience, including disease, defeat by enemies, and exile. **Ezekiel 18:20**, says, "*The soul who sins shall die.*" This highlights personal responsibility for breaking God's laws, including the commandments. **Deuteronomy 5:9-10**, speaks about God's judgment: "*I, the Lord your God, am a jealous God, punishing the children for the sin of the parents to the third and fourth generation of those who hate me.*"

Remember all the other laws in the Bible? Well, these laws said if you sin, bring a sacrifice to the priest for forgiveness. The word SIN was used over and over and over again. In the New Testament, I will show you how to bypass the priest and how Jesus' atonement was more permanent.

KEY: When the 10 Commandments were given to Moses, every command had a consequence. The consequence resulted in an action, meaning that something is going to happen to you if you do it.

For instance, to observe the Sabbath day by keeping it holy. As a result, **Exodus 35:2** says, "*Anyone who works on that day must be put to death.*" I believe what God is saying here is that if you disobey my command, you have sinned because you know the difference between right and wrong; therefore, you will die. Die means to die without God after this life.

While there were consequences for disobeying God's commands, there were also benefits for obedience. God did this because despite their sins, He still loved them. Remember the 5th commandment? The promise for honoring your parents is you will live a long life. Not only was there a blessing in honoring your parents, but there were also so many promises of blessings in Deuteronomy 28 for obedience.

Those promises of Deuteronomy 28:2-14 were:

2 And all these blessings shall come on thee, and overtake thee, if thou shalt hearken unto the voice of the Lord thy God.

3 Blessed shalt thou be in the city, and blessed shalt thou be in the field.

4 Blessed shall be the fruit of thy body, and the fruit of thy ground, and the fruit of thy cattle, the increase of thy kine, and the flocks of thy sheep.

5 Blessed shall be thy basket and thy store.

6 Blessed shalt thou be when thou comest in, and blessed shalt thou be when thou goest out.

7 The Lord shall cause thine enemies that rise up against thee to be smitten before thy face: they shall come out against thee one way, and flee before thee seven ways.

8 The Lord shall command the blessing upon thee in thy storehouses, and in all that thou settest thine hand unto; and he shall bless thee in the land which the Lord thy God giveth thee.

9 The Lord shall establish thee an holy people unto himself, as he hath sworn unto thee, if thou shalt keep the commandments of the Lord thy God, and walk in his ways.

10 And all people of the earth shall see that thou art called by the name of the Lord; and they shall be afraid of thee.

11 And the Lord shall make thee plenteous in goods, in the fruit of thy body, and in the fruit of thy cattle, and in the fruit of thy ground, in the land which the Lord sware unto thy fathers to give thee.

12 The Lord shall open unto thee his good treasure, the heaven to give the rain unto thy land in his season, and to bless all the work of thine hand: and thou shalt lend unto many nations, and thou shalt not borrow.

13 And the Lord shall make thee the head, and not the tail; and thou shalt be above only, and thou shalt not be beneath; if that thou hearken unto the commandments of the Lord thy God, which I command thee this day, to observe and to do them:

14 And thou shalt not go aside from any of the words which I command thee this day, to the right hand, or to the left, to go after other gods to serve them.

There were so many promises of blessings for obedience, but way more consequences of disobedience that come in the form of curses. **Deuteronomy 28:15-68** lists all these curses, which ended with being put back into slavery on ships for disobedience. Sounds like those who were enslaved in America, right? Yeah, that is another conversation, so we will leave that right there.

The main points I want to drive home is that the 10 commandments were meant to give our life order, structure and holiness like God. When we sin, disobey His commandments, and walk contrary to his laws and statutes, we will remain in perpetual disconnection from Him, His presence and His benefits.

The Ten Commandments are far more than a historical list of divine decrees; they are a timeless framework for living a life that honors God and reflects His holiness. These commandments not only guide moral conduct but also reveal the depth of God's character and our need for His grace.

Through Christ, we are empowered by the Holy Spirit to fulfill the heart of these commandments—loving God and loving others **(Matthew 22:37-40)**. While we are no longer bound by the law for salvation, its principles remain essential as a compass for righteous living and a reminder of our calling to be set apart in a world longing for truth. By aligning our lives with the spirit of these commands, we bear witness to the transformative power of God's Word and walk in the abundant life He intended for His people.

PATRICIA S. TANNER

Chapter 4

The Story Of The Prophets

The first five books of the Bible are called the TORAH or the Pentateuch, because they are the books of Moses. The themes of these books are parallel to the life of the believer.

First, we were created, then at some point in our life we are saved; then God sanctifies us. It's always Exodus before Leviticus, it's always salvation before sanctification. God always redeems His people before He asks anything from them. But sanctification isn't an upward process, there is always a lot of spiritual wandering and struggle.

Now, here we are in the land of Canaan. God was upset with the next generation. They did everything God told them *not* to do in this land. Sound familiar?

Moses spent his entire life trying to convince these people to listen to God and they experienced Gods wrath in the desert for being disobedient. Sounds familiar?

They had a new leader named Joshua who was led by God to help them conquer the promised land. They went into the land of Canaan, experienced all the spoils there, and still could not find total satisfaction in God, their creator.

The Israelites continued in their discontent and wanted to be like the other nations around them; now they wanted a king. They were tired of God, a Spirit, telling them what to do and how to live.

Sounds like my kids.

They wanted a physical human being to rule over them, as if God had not proven Himself with many years of miracles before. So, He gave them exactly what they wanted-He appointed King Saul to rule over them.

While God was loving and compassionate, King Saul was nothing like God. He saw a nation of people coming from the desert by the millions and he was intimidated by the number of people. He heard that God was with them, and they were healthy and strong people. He decided to take the people and enslave them to work the land. He held them in captivity until they cried out to God to rescue them. God heard their cries and rescued them once again from the hands of King Saul.

Before I get into detail about the prophets, I do not want you to miss the book called Judges. I will not go into detail, but I will give you an overview. The book of Judges talked about a lot of judges who ruled over the Israelites. This book will show you how God's people prospered and did very well, but they forgot about God; so, they suffered. Then they turned their backs to God and prospered again. Every time they turned their backs to God, God appointed a better Judge who ruled over them.

Can you imagine?

The repeat disobedience to God and then the rescue; God was fed up. This is the story of the Prophets. These books of the Prophets begin with Joshua, all the way to Malachi. Joshua's role was to settle the Israelites in Canaan (the promised land) and teach them about the word of God. That failed.

Moses couldn't do it, and Joshua wasn't all that convincing to them either. God replaced King Saul with King David who rose into power because the Prophet Samuel was called by God to tell David to rule over His nation. Get ready for the rollercoaster.

The Israelites could not decide whom they should worship. God sent prophet after prophet after prophet to speak to them about an announcement and preparation of the coming of a King. This King that was coming to save them was God Himself from heaven to Earth to rescue His people from oppression.

Wow, what a mighty GOD we serve! Don't take my word for it. I can prove it based on the following scriptures I mentioned from the Bible. You must have an open mind because remember I said it is a 'prophecy.' The definition of prophecy in a nutshell is to see ahead and say what was seen. You get the point.

What you must understand about the prophets who were assigned to the children of Israel, is that they endured much strife and hardship to deliver their messages. It was never an easy feat to tell a rebellious group of people that they needed to change their ways, depart from idols, or return to God's commandments.

The Prophets Through The Word

The accomplishments of the prophets were not just to speak the oracles of God, but to ensure those oracles returned the people to a relationship with God. This was done to bring them to repentance and introduce the New Covenant into the Earth. Throughout history, the prophets prophesied the coming of the Messiah who would pronounce the final redemption of man.

Isaiah 7:14 says, *"All right then, the Lord Himself will give you the sign. Look! The virgin will conceive a child! She will give birth to a son and will call Him Immanuel (which means 'God is with us')."*

Hmmmmm, I wonder who that will be……

Isaiah 9:6-7 says, *"For a child is born to us, a son is given to us. The government will rest on His shoulders. And He will be called: Wonderful Counselor, Mighty God, Everlasting Father, Prince of Peace. His government and its peace will never end. He will rule with fairness and justice from the throne of his ancestor David for all eternity. The passionate commitment of the Lord of Heaven's Armies will make this happen!"*

Are you convinced yet?

Isaiah 11:1-5 says, *"Out of the stump of David's family will grow a shoot— yes, a new Branch bearing fruit from the old root. And the Spirit of the Lord will rest on Him—the Spirit of wisdom and understanding, the Spirit of counsel and might, the Spirit of knowledge and the fear of the Lord. He will delight in obeying the Lord. He will not judge by appearance nor make a decision based on hearsay. He will give justice to the poor and make fair decisions for the exploited. The earth will shake at the force of His word, and one breath from His mouth will destroy the wicked. He will wear righteousness like a belt and truth like an undergarment."*

Open your mind and heart.

The answer to whom this person is will be revealed in the next few chapters.

Micah 5:2-3 says, *"But you, O Bethlehem Ephrathah, are only a small village among all the people of Judah. Yet a ruler of Israel, whose origins are in the distant past, will come from you on my behalf. The people of Israel will be abandoned to their enemies until the woman in labor gives birth. Then at last his fellow countrymen will return from exile to their own land."*

I am about to shout all by myself…….

Zechariah 9:9 says, *"Rejoice, O people of Zion! Shout in triumph, O people of Jerusalem! Look, your king is coming to you. He is righteous and victorious, yet He is humble, riding on a donkey—riding on a donkey's colt."*

Now the Spirit should be working in you to reveal this mystery. Who is this King I say?

Malachi 3:1 says, *"Look! I am sending my messenger, and he will prepare the way before me. Then the Lord you are seeking will suddenly come to His Temple. The messenger of the covenant, whom you look for so eagerly, is surely coming," says the Lord of Heaven's Armies."*

Ok you Religious Leaders, by now, the truth should be revealed.

Isaiah 61:1 says, *"The Spirit of the Sovereign Lord is upon me, for the Lord has anointed me to bring good news to the poor. He has sent me to comfort the brokenhearted and to proclaim that captives will be released, and prisoners will be freed."*

Does this sound like somebody you know in the New Testament yet? In the end, the vast majority of believers will die before they enter the promised land, like in the old days. But what matters in the end, is that they remain faithful to God's covenant.

The prophets served as God's messengers, faithfully proclaiming His word and pointing toward the coming of the Messiah, Jesus Christ. Their writings and prophecies unveil a divine tapestry, woven with themes of hope, redemption, and restoration. From Isaiah's vision of the suffering servant to Micah's pinpointing of Bethlehem as the Messiah's birthplace, every prophetic utterance spoke of God's unchanging plan to redeem humanity through His Son.

Numbers 24:17 says, *"I see him, but not here and now. I perceive him, but far in the distant future. A star will rise from Jacob; a scepter will emerge from Israel. It will crush the heads of Moab's people, cracking the skulls of the people of Sheth."*

Deuteronomy 18:15 says, *"Moses continued, "The Lord your God will raise up for you a prophet like me from among your fellow Israelites. You must listen to him."*

Jesus' life, death, and resurrection are the ultimate fulfillment of these prophecies, confirming the faithfulness of God's promises and the reliability of His Word and the fulfillment of His covenants. As believers, the prophetic messages not only deepen our understanding of Christ's mission but also strengthen our faith in His return and the completion of God's redemptive plan.

The prophets remind us that history is not random; it is sovereignly directed toward the glorious day when every knee will bow, and every tongue confess that Jesus is Lord. Their voices echo through the ages, inviting us to trust in the Messiah and live in the hope of His ultimate victory.

As we explore the birth of Christ, I need you to keep these prophetic utterances of His coming from the prophets. You should be jumping for joy because the new covenant is going to be revealed, which rings with the theme of this book: SALVATION-your ticket into heaven.

Chapter 5

The Birth Of Jesus

And the Word was made flesh, and dwelt among us, (and we beheld his glory, the glory as of the only begotten of the Father,) full of grace and truth.

-John 1:14 (KJV)

Long ago, in a small village called Nazareth, there lived a young woman named Mary. She was kind and humble, betrothed to a carpenter named Joseph.

One quiet evening, as Mary went about her tasks, an angel named Gabriel appeared to her, shining with heavenly light. "Greetings, favored one!" Gabriel announced. "The Lord is with you!"

Mary, startled and unsure, listened as the angel continued. "Do not be afraid, Mary. You have found favor with God. You will conceive and give birth to a son, and you will name Him Jesus. He will be very great and will be called the Son of the Most High. The Lord God will give Him the

> *And the angel came in unto her, and said, Hail, thou that art highly favored, the Lord is with thee: blessed art thou among women.*
> **~Luke 1:28**

throne of His ancestor David, and He will reign over Israel forever. His kingdom will never end."

Mary, though young, was faithful. She asked, "How can this happen? I am a virgin."

The angel replied, "The Holy Spirit will come upon you, and the power of the Most High will overshadow you. So, the baby to be born will be holy, and He will be called the Son of God. For nothing is impossible with God."

With reverence and trust, Mary responded, "I am the Lord's servant. May everything you have said about me come true."

And with that, the angel left her. Nine months later, at night, under the canopy of stars, Mary gave birth to her firstborn son in Bethlehem in Judea, during the reign of King Herod. His name was Jesus. The promised Messiah had arrived—the Savior of the world.

I wanted to introduce you to Jesus. The prophecy of His coming was fulfilled. The baby was born.

Do you recall in the last chapter that we visited this prophecy? According to the scripture, **Isaiah 7:14** *says, "All right then, the Lord himself will give you the sign. Look! The virgin will conceive a child! She will give birth to a son and will call Him Immanuel (which means 'God is with us')."*

An angel appeared to Joseph in a dream about Jesus being born (**Matthew 1:20-23**). The Bible really doesn't speak about Jesus growing up from a baby to the age of 12. But according to the prophet Isaiah, looks like God was preparing Him to rescue the world.

Isaiah 9:6-7 says, *"For a child is born to us, a son is given to us. The government will rest on His shoulders. And He will be called: Wonderful Counselor, Mighty God, Everlasting Father, Prince of Peace. His government and its peace will never end. He will rule with fairness and justice from the throne of His ancestor David for all eternity. The passionate commitment of the Lord of Heaven's Armies will make this happen!"*

Remember this scripture, **Micah 5:2-3** *says, "But you, O Bethlehem Ephrathah, are only a small village among all the people of Judah.*

Yet a ruler of Israel, whose origins are in the distant past, will come from you on my behalf. The people of Israel will be abandoned to their enemies until the woman in labor gives birth. Then at last His fellow countrymen will return from exile to their own land."

In Chapter one, I asked the question, "Who is God?" To answer the question, I described him as a Spirit. I also said that God made us in His image and likeness. We are triune beings with a spirit, body, and soul. If we were made like Him, then we look like Him. God is a spirit, body, and soul.

The birth of Jesus mentions that Mary was a virgin. Everyone knows what a virgin is, right? I don't have to break that down to you. However, we know that a female body can conceive a baby.

The angel told Mary, "The Holy Spirit will come upon you, and the power of the Most High will overshadow you." Sounds to me like the Spirit of God was manifesting Himself through a virgin to go into a body. The body that was conceived was called Jesus.

When you look in the mirror, do you see a body? What is your body called? Mine is called Patricia and I am called 'daughter.' Therefore, God called His body Jesus, which is called 'son.'

When a man and woman have a child, whether a male or female, it is called son or daughter. Well, Jesus' body is called son. You don't have to have a title to understand simple context. However, you do have to have common sense.

KEY: If you listen to Jesus, He mentioned the scriptures to the religious leaders. In **Matthew 22:29-32**, "Jesus replied, *"Your mistake is that you don't know the scriptures, and you don't know the power of God. For when the dead rise, they will neither marry nor be given in marriage. In this respect they will be like the angels in heaven. "But now, as to whether there will be a resurrection of the dead—haven't you ever read about this in the Scriptures? Long* *after Abraham, Isaac, and Jacob had died, God said, 'I am the God of Abraham, the God of Isaac, and the God of Jacob.' So, He is the God of the living, not the dead."*

The Destiny Of Christ

As we explore Christ, we cannot stop at His birth. We must move forward into His sinless life, sacrificial death and resurrection to reign in power with our Father. Jesus played such an amazing role in humanity that His name is still famous some 2,000+ years later. Let's take a quick dive into these aspects of His life.

1. The Birth of Jesus: Fulfillment of Prophecy

- **Virgin Birth:** Jesus was born of a virgin, fulfilling Isaiah's prophecy (*"The virgin will conceive and give birth to a son, and will call him Immanuel"* - **Isaiah 7:14; Matthew 1:23**). His miraculous birth confirmed His divine nature and identity as the Son of God.

- **Bethlehem as the Prophesied Location:** His birth in Bethlehem fulfilled **Micah 5:2**, establishing His Messianic legitimacy.

- **Divine Purpose:** The angel's announcement to Mary and Joseph revealed His mission: *"He will save his people from their sins"* (**Matthew 1:21**).

2. His Life: The Perfect Example of Holiness

- **Sinless Life:** Jesus lived a life without sin, perfectly fulfilling the law (**Hebrews 4:15**). His obedience set Him apart as the only suitable sacrifice for the sins of humanity.

- **Teacher and Miracle Worker:** Through His teachings, parables, and miracles, Jesus revealed the nature of God, demonstrated His authority, and showed compassion for humanity.

  - *Examples:* Healing the sick, raising the dead, feeding the multitudes, and calming the storm.

  - *"The Son of Man came to seek and save the lost"* (**Luke 19:10**).

- **Revealing the Kingdom of God:** His life emphasized repentance, faith, and the coming kingdom, inviting people into a relationship with God (**Mark 1:15**).

---

3. His Death: The Atoning Sacrifice

- **Prophecies Fulfilled:** Jesus' death was foretold by prophets like Isaiah, who described Him as the suffering servant (*"He was pierced for our transgressions, he was crushed for our iniquities"* - **Isaiah 53:5**).

- **The Crucifixion:** Jesus willingly endured the cross, taking upon Himself the punishment for sin that humanity deserved (**1 Peter 2:24**).

- **Substitutionary Atonement:** His death paid the price for sin, satisfying God's justice while demonstrating His love (*"God demonstrates his own love for us in this: While we were still sinners, Christ died for us"* - **Romans 5:8**).

- **The Veil Torn in Two:** The tearing of the temple veil at His death symbolized the removal of the barrier between God and humanity (**Matthew 27:51**).

---

4. His Resurrection: Victory Over Sin and Death

- **Fulfillment of His Promise:** Jesus' resurrection on the third day validated His claims to be the Son of God and the Savior of the world (*"He is not here; he has risen, just as He said"* - **Matthew 28:6**).

- **Victory Over Death:** By rising from the dead, Jesus defeated the power of sin and death, offering eternal life to all who believe (**1 Corinthians 15:54-57**).

- **Hope for Believers:** The resurrection assures believers of their own resurrection and eternal life in heaven (**1 Thessalonians 4:14**).

---

5. The Birth, Life, Death, and Resurrection in Salvation

- **Salvation Through Faith:** Jesus' entire mission—from His birth to His resurrection—provides the foundation for salvation. *"If you declare with your mouth, 'Jesus is Lord,'* *and believe in your heart that God raised Him from the dead, you will be saved"* (**Romans 10:9**).

- **Grace, Not Works:** His sacrificial work underscores that salvation is a gift of grace, not something earned by human effort (**Ephesians 2:8-9**).

- **Access to Heaven:** Through Jesus, believers are justified, reconciled to God, and assured a place in heaven (**John 14:6**).

---

6. Practical Application for Believers

- **Trust in His Finished Work:** Salvation is found in Christ alone. His birth, life, death, and resurrection are proof of God's faithfulness to redeem His people.

- **Share the Gospel:** Understanding Jesus' mission compels Christians to share the Good News of salvation with others (**Matthew 28:19-20**).

- **Live in Hope:** The resurrection gives believers hope and confidence in eternal life, shaping how they live today with faith, love, and purpose.

The birth of Jesus is the ultimate display of God's love for humanity, setting in motion the events that would lead to redemption and eternal life. His sinless life revealed the standard of holiness, His death paid the penalty for sin, and His resurrection conquered death once and for all. Through Him, salvation is not only possible but assured for those who believe in securing their place in heaven.

All of this explains that God is of the living and sin is of the dead. MY GOD!!! Therefore, when you sin, you die. I just summed up all the keys to this point. There's more at the end of the book. Just keep reading and paying attention.

A sinless man had to be born to save us. Ok, now I'm done talking, let's go to the next chapter.

PATRICIA S. TANNER

Chapter 6

The 12 Disciples

One day as Jesus was standing by the Lake of Gennesaret the people were crowding around him and listening to the word of God. He saw at the water's edge two boats, left there by the fishermen, who were washing their nets. He got into one of the boats, the one belonging to Simon, and asked him to put out a little from shore. Then he sat down and taught the people from the boat.

-Luke 5:1-3 (NIV)

The twelve disciples, also known as the apostles, were ordinary men called by Jesus for an extraordinary purpose. They were fishermen, tax collectors, and common laborers—diverse in background yet unified by Christ's transformative call: *"Follow me, and I will make you fishers of men"* (**Matthew 4:19**). These men were chosen not for their qualifications but for their willingness to leave everything behind and embrace a life of faith, learning, and service under Jesus' teaching.

In their time with Jesus, the disciples witnessed miracles, heard the wisdom of heaven, and participated in the ministry of the Messiah. Their lives were forever changed as they transitioned from being students of Christ to becoming His sent ones, tasked with spreading the Gospel to the ends of the earth. While they were not perfect—struggling with doubt, fear, and even betrayal—their journey illustrates God's ability to work through flawed individuals to accomplish His divine plan.

This chapter explores the lives of the twelve disciples: their call, their relationship with Jesus, their roles in His ministry, and the legacy they left behind. By examining their stories, we can uncover valuable lessons about obedience, faith, and the power of God to use the willing to fulfill His mission. Let us delve into their lives and reflect on how their calling echoes in the mission of every believer today.

Here are the names of the disciples and their importance:

1. *Simon Peter (Cephas)*

   • **Role:** Leader among the disciples.

   • **Details:** A fisherman by trade, Peter was often outspoken and impulsive but deeply devoted. Jesus referred to him as the "rock" on which He would build His church (**Matthew 16:18**). Peter became a prominent leader in the early Christian church and was instrumental in spreading the gospel, especially to the Jewish community.

2. *Andrew*
   - **Role:** Evangelist and introducer.
   - **Details:** Peter's brother and a fisherman, Andrew was the one who brought Peter to Jesus (**John 1:41**). He was known for bringing others to Christ and played a role in spreading the gospel.

3. *James (Son of Zebedee)*
   - **Role:** One of the "Sons of Thunder" and an early martyr.
   - **Details:** Along with his brother John, James was part of Jesus' inner circle. He witnessed key moments, such as

The Transfiguration. He was the first apostle to be martyred for his faith (**Acts 12:1-2**).

4. *John (Son of Zebedee)*
   - **Role:** "The disciple whom Jesus loved."
   - **Details:** John was part of the inner circle with Peter and James. He is traditionally credited with writing the Gospel of John, three epistles (**1 John, 2 John, 3 John**), and Revelation. He emphasized love and truth in his teachings.

5. *Philip*
   - **Role:** Questioner and facilitator.
   - **Details:** Philip was known for bringing others to Jesus, including Nathanael (**John 1:45-46**). He often asked practical questions that allowed Jesus to explain deeper truths.

6. *Bartholomew (Nathanael)*
   - **Role:** A seeker of truth.
   - **Details:** Known for his honesty and faith, Jesus described him as "an Israelite indeed, in whom is no deceit" (**John 1:47**). Tradition holds that he became a missionary and was martyred.

7. *Matthew (Levi)*
   - **Role:** Tax collector turned disciple and Gospel writer.
   - **Details:** Matthew worked as a tax collector before following Jesus, a profession despised by Jews. He is credited with writing the Gospel of Matthew and was known for emphasizing Jesus as the fulfillment of Old Testament prophecies.

8. *Thomas (Didymus)*
   - **Role:** Skeptic turned faithful believer.
   - **Details:** Often remembered as "Doubting Thomas" because he questioned Jesus' resurrection until he saw and touched His wounds (**John 20:24-29**). He later showed great faith and is believed to have carried the gospel to India.

9. *James (Son of Alphaeus)*
   - **Role:** Often referred to as "James the Less."
   - **Details:** Not much is known about James, but he is distinguished from James, son of Zebedee. He faithfully followed Jesus and contributed to the spread of Christianity.

10. *Thaddaeus (Judas, Son of James)*
    - **Role:** Also called "Jude."
    - **Details:** He asked Jesus about why He would reveal Himself to the disciples but not to the world (**John 14:22**). He is traditionally associated with the Epistle of Jude and missionary work.

11. *Simon the Zealot*
    - **Role**: Zealot turned disciple.
    - **Details**: Simon likely belonged to a revolutionary Jewish group before following Jesus. His zeal for God was redirected toward spreading the gospel.

12. *Judas Iscariot*
    - **Role:** Treasurer and betrayer.
    - **Details:** Judas was responsible for managing the group's finances but later betrayed Jesus for 30 pieces of silver

(**Matthew 26:14-16**). After realizing his guilt, he took his own life (**Matthew 27:3-5**). After Judas Iscariot's betrayal and death, he was replaced by Matthias (**Acts 1:23-26**) to restore the group to 12 apostles. Each disciple played a foundational role in establishing and spreading the Christian faith.

You may ask yourself, why did Jesus pick these disciples. The purpose of Jesus choosing the disciples was multifaceted, reflecting His mission to reveal God's kingdom, establish the foundation of the church, and spread the message of salvation to the world.

Let me go more in depth. Jesus wanted them to learn from Him and witness His life. Jesus chose the disciples to be His closest companions, living and learning alongside Him during His earthly ministry. Through His teachings, miracles, and actions, they gained firsthand knowledge of God's character and mission.

Mark 3:14, says, "*He appointed twelve that they might be with Him and that He might send them out to preach.*"

Jesus picked them to assist in His ministry. The disciples helped Jesus during His public ministry by ministering to people, distributing food during miracles (e.g., feeding the 5,000), and preparing for His travels.

Luke 10:1, says, "*After this, the Lord appointed seventy-two others and sent them two by two ahead of Him to every town and place where he was about to go.*"

This reason is a big one.

Jesus wanted them to spread the Gospel. He trained the disciples to continue His mission after His death and resurrection. They were to proclaim the good news of salvation, starting in Jerusalem and extending to the ends of the earth. **Matthew 28:19**, says, "*Go and make disciples of all the nations, baptizing them in the name of the Father and the Son and the Holy Spirit.*"

He did it to establish the foundation of the church. The disciples were the foundational leaders of the early Christian Church, responsible for teaching, preaching, and guiding the first communities of believers.

Ephesians 2:20, says, "*Together, we are His house, built on the foundation of the apostles and the prophets. And the cornerstone is Christ Jesus Himself.*"

Jesus wanted to demonstrate the power of transformation. Jesus chose individuals from diverse and sometimes flawed backgrounds (e.g., fishermen, a tax collector, a zealot) to show that God can transform ordinary people into extraordinary messengers of His kingdom. This demonstrated that His message was for everyone.

1 Corinthians 1:26 says, "*Brothers and sisters, think of what you were when you were called. Not many of you were wise by human standards; not many were influential; not many were of noble birth.*"

Jesus exemplified servant leadership to the disciples, teaching them humility, love, and sacrifice. He instructed them to follow His example in their leadership roles.

Matthew 20:26-28, says, *"Whoever wants to be a leader among you must be your servant, and whoever wants to be first among you must become your slave. For even the Son of Man came not to be served but to serve others and to give his life as a ransom for many."*

Last but not least, Jesus chose the disciples to witness Jesus' death and resurrection and testify to its truth. Their eyewitness accounts became the basis of the gospel message.

Acts 1:8, says, *"You will be my witnesses, telling people about me everywhere—in Jerusalem, throughout Judea, in Samaria, and to the ends of the earth."*

Through these chosen individuals, Jesus ensured the continuation of His mission and the spread of His message to future generations. The disciples' work laid the groundwork for Christianity, which continues to thrive worldwide. Now that you know who they are, you will know throughout the New Testament how Jesus worked with each of them.

Chapter 7

The Jewish Religious Leaders

Be shepherds of God's flock that is under your care, watching over them—not because you must, but because you are willing, as God wants you to be; not pursuing dishonest gain, but eager to serve; not lording it over those entrusted to you, but being examples to the flock. And when the Chief Shepherd appears, you will receive the crown of glory that will never fade away.

-I Peter 5:2-4 (NIV)

The New Testament mentions various religious leaders who played key roles during Jesus' ministry and the early church period. These leaders were often connected to Jewish religious institutions. I wanted you know who they were and the roles and positions they played when Jesus was here on earth.

Jewish Religious Leaders

1. Pharisees

◦ **Who They Were**: A prominent religious group who followed the Law of Moses and oral traditions. They were influential in synagogues and among the Jewish people.

◦ *Role:* Teachers of the law, interpreters of Scripture, and promoters of piety.

◦ *Key Figures:*

▪ **Nicodemus:** A Pharisee who came to Jesus by night seeking truth **(John 3:1-21).**

- **Paul (Saul of Tarsus):** A Pharisee before his conversion to Christianity (**Philippians 3:5**).

2. Sadducees

Who They Were: A priestly and aristocratic group that held significant power in the temple and among the ruling elite. They rejected beliefs not explicitly found in the Torah, such as the resurrection of the dead.

Role: Controlled the Temple rituals and served on the Sanhedrin, the Jewish ruling council.

Key Figures: Often unnamed but opposed Jesus and the apostles, especially regarding the resurrection (**Acts 4:1-2**).

3. Scribes

Who They Were: Experts in the Law who copied, interpreted, and taught the Scriptures.

Role: Legal scholars and advisors to the Pharisees and Sadducees.

Key Figures: Frequently mentioned in opposition to Jesus, as they were critical of His interpretations of the law (Mark 12:38-40).

4. High Priests

Who They Were: Leaders of the temple worship, responsible for offering sacrifices and overseeing religious ceremonies.

Role: Represented the people before God and led the Sanhedrin.

Key Figures:

Caiaphas: The high priest during Jesus' trial and crucifixion (**Matthew 26:57**).

Annas: Caiaphas' father-in-law and influential in Jewish religious affairs (**John 18:13**).

5. *Sanhedrin*

<u>**Who They Were:**</u> The ruling council of Jewish leaders, composed of Pharisees, Sadducees, and scribes.

Role: Judicial and legislative authority over Jewish religious and civil matters. They tried Jesus and later persecuted His followers (**Matthew 26:59, Acts 5:27-28**).

Jesus was often angry with the Pharisees and Sadducees because their behavior, teachings, and attitudes were contrary to God's will and the heart of true faith. Jesus felt like they were hypocrites and had a lack of integrity.

The Pharisees emphasized outward religious practices but neglected inner righteousness and genuine love for God and others. They often acted pious to gain public admiration while their hearts were far from God.

Jesus says, *"What sorrow awaits you teachers of religious law and you Pharisees. Hypocrites! For you are like whitewashed tombs—beautiful on the outside but filled on the inside with dead people's bones and all sorts of impurity"* (**Matthew 23:27, NLT**). They were burdening the people with legalism.

The Pharisees added countless man-made rules and traditions to God's law, making it difficult for people to follow. They focused on minor details while neglecting justice, mercy, and faith. Jesus says, *"For you crush people with unbearable religious demands, and you never lift a finger to ease the burden"* (**Luke 11:46 NLT**).

The Pharisees and the Sadducees had a lot of pride, and they were self-righteous. Both groups were often arrogant, viewing themselves as morally and spiritually superior to others. This blinded them to their need for repentance and the grace of God. Jesus says, *"For those who exalt themselves will be humbled, and those who humble themselves will be exalted"* (**Luke 18:14, NLT**).

The Pharisees and Sadducees used their religious authority for personal gain. They exploited the poor, sought wealth and power, and corrupted the Temple system with practices like dishonest money changing. Jesus got angry and drove out the money changers from the Temple, saying, *"The Scriptures declare, 'My Temple will be called a house of prayer,' but you have turned it into a den of thieves!"* (**Matthew 21:13, NLT**). They despised Jesus and His teachings. Both groups refused to acknowledge Jesus as the Messiah despite the evidence of His miracles and teachings. Their hard hearts and spiritual blindness caused them to reject the very one they claimed to serve.

Jesus says, *"You search the Scriptures because you think they give you eternal life. But the Scriptures point to me! Yet you refuse to come to me to receive this life"* (**John 5:39-40, NLT**). The Pharisees and Sadducees prioritized strict adherence to rules over compassion and mercy. For example, they criticized Jesus for healing on the Sabbath instead of rejoicing in God's power to bring healing.

Jesus says, *"You would not have condemned my innocent disciples if you knew the meaning of this Scripture: 'I want you to show mercy, not offer sacrifices'"* (**Matthew 12:7, NLT**). As leaders, they had a responsibility to guide people toward God. Instead, they led them astray with false teachings and their bad example.

Jesus says, *"What sorrow awaits you teachers of religious law and you Pharisees. Hypocrites! For you shut the door of the*

Kingdom of Heaven in people's faces. You won't go in yourselves, and you don't let others enter either" (**Matthew 23:13, NLT**). I want you to feel the anger from these religious leaders. They were more stuck on religion than belief. They could not understand why Jesus was hanging around sinners and spreading the gospel. It was against their tradition and laws of the land. They could not wrap their head around the fact that there was a possibility He *was* the Messiah.

All in all, Jesus' anger stemmed from His love for truth, justice, and the people the Pharisees and Sadducees were misleading. He sought to correct their errors and call them to repentance, but their pride and resistance ultimately led to His condemnation of their actions.

Religious Leaders Of Today

Primarily in the scriptures, Jesus addresses the religious leaders of His day. But this does not exempt the application of these scriptures to today's leaders. Let's take a brief look at the reoccurring themes with leadership that would be relevant to today.

By comparing Jesus' approach to the religious leaders of His time with how He might address modern religious leaders, we can draw valuable insights into the consistent principles of His ministry and His expectations for those who shepherd His people.

Confronting Hypocrisy

Jesus was a master at confronting hypocrisy. He repeatedly called out religious leaders for their hypocrisy, accusing them of presenting an outward appearance of righteousness while harboring corruption within. He likened them to whitewashed tombs—beautiful on the outside but full of dead men's bones inside (**Matthew 23:27-28**). They focused on ceremonial observances and public displays of piety while neglecting weightier matters of the law, such as justice and mercy.

In today's society, Jesus might similarly confront modern leaders who prioritize appearances, wealth, or institutional power over authentic spirituality and service. Leaders who preach holiness but fail to practice it themselves, or who exploit their positions for personal gain, would face the same rebuke. God values integrity of heart over superficial religiosity. Leaders must lead by example, living out the faith they proclaim.

Exposing Spiritual Pride

Exposing spiritual pride was part of Jesus's main agenda to establish order in the earth. Religious leaders sought recognition, sitting in seats of honor and enjoying titles that elevated their status (**Matthew 23:5-7**). Their pride prevented them from acknowledging their need for repentance and blinded them to Jesus as the Messiah.

In modern times, leaders who build ministries around their personalities, crave celebrity status, or refuse accountability might face similar correction. Jesus would remind them that leadership is a calling to serve, not to be served (**Mark 10:42-45**). True greatness in the kingdom of God is measured by humility and servanthood, not by fame or influence.

Focusing On The Heart Of Worship

Jesus rebuked leaders who turned the temple into a marketplace, prioritizing profit over worship (**Matthew 21:12-13**). He reminded them that God desires worship in spirit and truth (**John 4:24**).

Jesus might confront leaders today who allow commercialism or worldly influences to overshadow genuine worship. Churches that prioritize entertainment or profit over discipleship might draw His critique. Worship is sacred and must center on glorifying God, not human agendas or material gain.

Extending Grace & Truth

Despite His rebukes, Jesus offered grace to leaders like Nicodemus and Joseph of Arimathea, who sought the truth with sincere hearts (**John 3:1-21; John 19:38-42**). His goal was not to condemn but to lead them into repentance and restoration.

Jesus would still extend grace to modern leaders who humbly recognize their shortcomings and seek His guidance. His rebukes are always an invitation to return to the heart of God. Leadership in God's kingdom is not about perfection but about humility, repentance, and a commitment to God's will.

Whether addressing the Pharisees of His day or modern religious leaders, Jesus' message remains the same: authentic faith is marked by humility, love, and obedience to God. He values leaders who shepherd His people with integrity, serve the vulnerable, and guide others into a genuine relationship with Him. The religious leaders of today are called to reflect Christ's example by prioritizing the things that matter most to God—justice, mercy, faithfulness, and a heart devoted to worship.

Chapter 8

The Fulfillment Of The Laws

For Christ is the end of the law for righteousness to everyone who believes.

-Romans 10:4 (ESV)

The fulfillment of the laws in the Bible is primarily found in the teachings and work of Jesus Christ in the New Testament. In the Gospel of Matthew, Jesus makes a clear statement about His relationship to the Law when He says, *"Do not think that I have come to abolish the law or the Prophets; I have not come to abolish them but to fulfill them"* (**Matthew 5:17, NIV**).

In this verse, Jesus is clarifying that His mission is not to discard or destroy the laws given in the Old Testament, but to complete or bring them to their intended fulfillment. He emphasizes that the Law (Torah) and the teachings of the Prophets are still significant. This is why I took you on a journey through the prophets, the disciples and ALMOST everything in between. He came to fulfill the purpose of the laws by living them out perfectly, teaching their true meaning, and ultimately, through His death and resurrection, completing the work they pointed toward.

The Law, also known as the Torah, consisted of commandments and regulations given by God to the Israelites through Moses. It included moral laws, ceremonial laws, and civil laws meant to govern the lives of the Jewish people. Jesus' mission was not to invalidate these laws but to complete their purpose and reveal their full meaning.

We will briefly review the 10 commandments again and see how Jesus came to fulfill the law, not to destroy it. Some say the Old Testament is concealed and the New Testament is revealed.

These are the 10 commandments concealed in the Old Testament and revealed through the New Testament:

1. **OLD TESTAMENT**: **Exodus 20:2** says, "I am the Lord your God, who rescued you from the land of Egypt, the place of your slavery."

   NEW TESTAMENT: **Matthew 22:37 (NIV)** says, *"Love the Lord your God with all your heart and with all your soul and with all your mind."*

2. **OLD TESTAMENT**: **Exodus 20:3-6** says, *"You must not have any other god but me. You must not make for yourself an idol of any kind or an image of anything in the heavens or on the earth or in the sea. You must not bow down to them or worship them, for I, the Lord your God, am a jealous God who will not tolerate your affection for any other gods. I lay the sins of the parents upon their children; the entire family is affected—even children in the third and fourth generations of those who reject me. But I lavish unfailing love for a thousand generations on those who love me and obey my commands."*

   NEW TESTAMENT: **Matthew 6:24 (NIV)** says, *"No one can serve two masters. Either you will hate the one and love the other, or you will be devoted to the one and despise the other. You cannot serve both God and money."*

3. **OLD TESTAMENT**: **Exodus 20:7** says, *"You must not misuse the name of the Lord your God. The Lord will not let you go unpunished if you misuse his name."*

   NEW TESTAMENT: **Matthew 12:31-32 (NIV)** says, *"And so I tell you, every kind of sin and slander can be* *forgiven, but blasphemy against the Spirit will not be forgiven."*

4. **OLD TESTAMENT**: **Exodus 20:8-11** says, *"Remember to observe the Sabbath day by keeping it holy. You have six days each week for your ordinary work, but the seventh day is a Sabbath day of rest dedicated to the Lord your God. On that day no one in your household may do any work. This includes you, your sons and daughters, your male and female servants, your livestock, and any foreigners living among you. For in six days the Lord made the heavens, the earth, the sea, and everything in them; but on the seventh day he rested. That is why the Lord blessed the Sabbath day and set it apart as holy."*

NEW TESTAMENT: **Matthew 12:8 (NIV)** says, *"For the Son of Man is Lord of the Sabbath."* Jesus says in **Matthew 12:11-12 (NIV)**, *"He said to them, "If any of you has a sheep and it falls into a pit on the Sabbath, will you not take hold of it and lift it out? 12 How much more valuable is a person than a sheep! Therefore, it is lawful to do good on the Sabbath."*

5. **OLD TESTAMENT**: **Exodus 20:12** says, *"Honor your father and mother. Then you will live a long, full life in the land the Lord your God is giving you."*

NEW TESTAMENT: **Matthew 15:4 (NIV)** says, *"For God said, 'Honor your father and mother' and 'Anyone who kidnaps someone is to be put to death.'"* Jesus reaffirms the commandment to honor one's parents, emphasizing its importance as part of God's moral law.

6. <u>OLD TESTAMENT</u>: **Exodus 20:13** says, *"You must not murder."*

   <u>NEW TESTAMENT</u>: **Matthew 5:21-22 (NIV)** says, *"You have heard that it was said to people long ago, 'You shall not murder, and anyone who murders will be subject to judgment.' But I tell you that anyone who is angry with a brother or sister will be subject to judgment."*

7. <u>OLD TESTAMENT</u>: **Exodus 20:14** says, *"You must not commit adultery."*

   <u>NEW TESTAMENT</u>: **Matthew 5:27-28 (NIV)** says, *"You have heard that it was said, 'You shall not commit adultery.' But I tell you that anyone who looks at a woman lustfully has already committed adultery with her in his heart."*

8. <u>OLD TESTAMENT</u>: **Exodus 20:15** says, *"You must not steal."*

   <u>NEW TESTAMENT</u>: **Matthew 19:18 (NIV)** says, *"You shall not murder, you shall not commit adultery, you shall not steal, you shall not give false testimony, honor your father and mother, and love your neighbor as yourself."*

9. <u>OLD TESTAMENT</u>: **Exodus 20:16** says, *"You must not testify falsely against your neighbor."*

   <u>NEW TESTAMENT</u>: **Matthew 5:25 (NIV)** says, *"Settle matters quickly with your adversary who is taking you to court. Do it while you are still together on the way, or your adversary may hand you over to the judge, and the judge may hand you over to the officer, and you may be thrown into prison."*

10. OLD TESTAMENT: **Exodus 20:17** says, *"You must not covet your neighbor's house. You must not covet your neighbor's wife, male or female servant, ox or donkey, or anything else that belongs to your neighbor."*

NEW TESTAMENT: **Luke 12:15 (NIV)** says, *"Watch out! Be on your guard against all kinds of greed; life does not consist in an abundance of possessions."* **James 2:10-13** says, *"For the person who keeps all of the laws except one is as guilty as a person who has broken all of God's laws. For the same God who said, "You must not commit adultery," also said, "You must not murder."*

If you murder someone but do not commit adultery, you have still broken the law. Whatever you say or whatever you do, remember that you will be judged by the law that sets you free. There will be no mercy for those who have not shown mercy to others. But if you have been merciful, God will be merciful when he judges you.

You see, Jesus did not change the law. He kept the law and added to it. One of the key ways Jesus fulfilled the law was by living a perfect life according to its standards. The law demanded perfection, but no human could fully obey all of it. Jesus, however, lived without sin, fulfilling the righteous requirements of the law that no one else could. He kept the commandments perfectly, demonstrating the true intent behind them, such as loving God with all one's heart and loving one's neighbor as oneself (**Matthew 22:37-40**). His life became the model for how to live in perfect obedience to God.

Moreover, Jesus' death on the cross was the ultimate fulfillment of the law's sacrificial system. The Old Testament law required the shedding of blood for the forgiveness of sins (**Leviticus**

17:11), and animal sacrifices were offered regularly. However, these sacrifices were temporary and pointed toward a greater sacrifice. Jesus, as the "Lamb of God," offered Himself as the once-and-for-all sacrifice for sin, fulfilling the law's demand for atonement (**Hebrews 10:12**). His death brought an end to the need for ongoing animal sacrifices, as He became the perfect and final offering.

Finally, the law's ultimate purpose was to point people to Christ, who would fulfill its righteous demands and offer salvation. The Apostle Paul explains this in **Galatians 3:24**, saying, *"So the law was our guardian until Christ came that we might be justified by faith."* The law revealed humanity's inability to perfectly obey and pointed toward the need for a Savior.

With Jesus' life, death, and resurrection, the law's purpose was fulfilled—not by its abolition, but by its completion in Christ, who offers forgiveness and righteousness through faith in Him. Thus, through Jesus, the law was not rendered obsolete but was *fulfilled* and transformed into a means of grace for all who believe.

I will end with this: **John 15:10 (NIV)** says, *"If you keep my commands, you will remain in my love, just as I have kept my Father's commands and remain in his love."*

PATRICIA S. TANNER

Chapter 9

They Killed The Messiah-Jesus Christ

For Christ also suffered once for sins, the righteous for the unrighteous, that he might bring us to God, being put to death in the flesh but made alive in the spirit.

-I Peter 3:18 (ESV)

The death of Jesus, as described in the New Testament, was a complex and deeply sorrowful event. The Jewish leaders of the time, including the Pharisees and the Sadducees, played a central role in orchestrating Jesus' crucifixion. They saw Him as a threat to their authority, as His teachings challenged the established religious order and His growing popularity among the people.

Jesus' claims to be the Son of God and the Messiah were considered blasphemous by these leaders. They had a narrow understanding of what the Messiah was supposed to be—primarily a political and military leader who would free them from Roman oppression. Because of this misunderstanding, they were blind to the true nature of His mission.

The Jews did not recognize Jesus as the Messiah because His arrival did not align with their expectations. They were expecting a triumphant king who would restore the kingdom of Israel, but Jesus came as a humble servant, preaching love, forgiveness, and repentance. His teachings were centered on a spiritual kingdom, not a political one. He healed the sick, performed miracles, and spoke of peace. Many saw these acts as too meek for someone claiming to be the Messiah.

Their inability to grasp the deeper meaning of Jesus' message, combined with their desire for a more immediate and tangible deliverance from Roman rule, led them to reject Him as the fulfillment of the Messianic prophecies. Despite their rejection of Jesus, His death on the cross was, paradoxically, part of God's plan for salvation. The Jewish leaders did not understand that His death was necessary for the atonement of sins, as outlined in the Old Testament scriptures.

Prophecies like those found in **Isaiah 53** pointed to a suffering servant who would be despised and rejected by His people. This was not the image they had in mind for the Messiah, but it was the image God had ordained for the Savior of the world. Jesus' death was the fulfillment of God's redemptive plan, providing a means for all humanity to be reconciled to God, including the very people who were complicit in His crucifixion. Even though the Jews of that time did not recognize Jesus as the Messiah, this act of rejection and crucifixion was ultimately a part of God's sovereign will.

In **Acts 3:17**, Peter addresses this misunderstanding by saying, *"Now, fellow Israelites, I know that you acted in ignorance, as did your leaders."* Many of those who were involved in Jesus' death did so out of a lack of understanding, not realizing they were fulfilling ancient prophecies that foretold the suffering of the Messiah. It wasn't until after His resurrection that many began to realize the truth—that Jesus was indeed the Messiah, and through His death and resurrection, the salvation of all people had been secured.

God's Plan For Humanity

The death of Jesus Christ stands at the very heart of God's plan for humanity's salvation. His crucifixion was not merely a tragic injustice or the result of political and religious hostility; it was the divine fulfillment of a plan conceived before the foundation of the world (**Revelation 13:8**).

Jesus willingly laid down His life as the ultimate sacrifice for sin, providing the only way for humanity to be reconciled with God and receive the promise of eternal life in heaven. We will examine the significance of His death, its relationship to salvation, and how it secures entry into heaven for all who believe.

There are 5 points relevant to salvation and what you need to take seriously for your entrance into the eternal kingdom:

1. The problem of sin (the need for salvation).
2. Jesus' death as the atoning sacrifice.
3. The relationship between death and salvation.
4. His death secures heaven for Believers.
5. The call to respond.
6. The victory of the cross.

Allow me to expound upon each of these five points:

The problem of sin.

Sin separates humanity from God, creating a spiritual chasm that no amount of human effort can bridge (**Isaiah 59:2; Romans 3:23**). God's holiness demands justice for sin, and the penalty for sin is death (**Romans 6:23**).

In the Old Testament, animal sacrifices temporarily atoned for sin, but they could not fully remove guilt or cleanse the human heart (**Hebrews 10:4**). Humanity needed a perfect, sinless sacrifice to satisfy God's justice and provide lasting redemption.

Jesus' death as the atoning sacrifice.

Jesus' death fulfilled His role as the Lamb of God, taking away the sin of the world (**John 1:29**). Unlike the sacrificial animals of the Old Covenant, His sacrifice was perfect and sufficient for all time (**Hebrews 10:10**).

Jesus died in our place, bearing the punishment for sin that we deserved. *"He was pierced for our transgressions, He was crushed for our iniquities; the punishment that brought us peace was on Him, and by His wounds, we are healed"* (**Isaiah 53:5**).

His death was foretold by prophets like Isaiah and Daniel, confirming that He was the Messiah sent to redeem humanity (**Isaiah 53:7-12; Daniel 9:26**).

The relationship between his death and salvation.

Jesus declared, *"It is finished"* (**John 19:30**) as He died, signifying that the debt of sin had been paid in full. Through His sacrifice, He satisfied God's wrath and secured forgiveness for all who believe (**Romans 5:9-11**).

The tearing of the temple veil at His death symbolized the removal of the barrier between God and humanity. Believers now have direct access to God through Jesus Christ (**Matthew 27:51; Hebrews 10:19-22**).

Salvation is a gift of God's grace, made possible through faith in Christ's finished work on the cross (**Ephesians 2:8-9**). Human effort or good deeds cannot earn salvation; it is entirely dependent on Jesus' death and resurrection.

His death secures heaven for believers.

Through Jesus' death, believers are justified—declared righteous before God (**2 Corinthians 5:21**). This reconciliation restores the relationship broken by sin and makes heaven a reality for those in Christ.

Jesus explicitly taught that He is the only way to the Father and to heaven. *"I am the way and the truth and the life. No one comes to the Father except through me"* (**John 14:6**). His death paved the way for believers to enter eternal fellowship with God.

Jesus' sacrifice not only removes sin but also grants eternal life. *"For God so loved the world that He gave His one and only Son, that whoever believes in Him shall not perish but have eternal life"* (**John 3:16**).

The call to respond.

To benefit from Jesus' sacrifice, individuals must respond in faith, believing that He died for their sins and rose again (**Romans 10:9-10**). Repentance—a turning away from sin and toward God—is an essential part of this response (**Acts 3:19**).

Baptism symbolizes a believer's union with Christ in His death, burial, and resurrection (**Romans 6:3-4**). While not a prerequisite for salvation, it is a step of obedience that reflects a transformed life.

The Victory Of The Cross

Jesus' death was not the end of the story. His resurrection on the third day demonstrated His victory over sin, death, and the grave (**1 Corinthians 15:54-57**). This victory assures believers that death is not the final word; eternal life awaits in heaven.

Jesus' death and resurrection also point to His second coming, when He will establish His eternal kingdom and bring full redemption to creation (**Revelation 21:1-4**).

Jesus' death was not a tragic accident but a divine necessity to accomplish salvation and secure the promise of heaven for all who believe. It satisfied God's justice, demonstrated His love, and opened the way for humanity to be reconciled with Him.

Through faith in the finished work of Christ, believers receive the assurance of forgiveness, peace with God, and the hope of eternal life. The cross is the ultimate expression of God's redemptive plan—a plan that guarantees salvation and a place in heaven for those who trust in Jesus as their Savior and Lord.

As we continue our journey exploring salvation, it is my hope and prayer that you will gain understanding of the path you take. You must take a path pleasing to God, and there is no other way to do that except through Jesus Christ.

We are not stopping at His death, it's time to receive the resurrected Christ! Onward Christian soldier!

PATRICIA S. TANNER

Chapter 10

The Resurrection-He Rose

God sent His Son, they called Him Jesus.

He came to love, heal and forgive.

He bled and died to buy my pardon.

An empty grave is there to prove

My Savior lives.

Because He lives, I can face tomorrow.

Because He lives all fear is gone.

Because I know He holds the future.

And life is worth living

Just because He lives.

-Lyrics from the song, 'Because He Lives.'

I began this chapter with a favored hymn because while it may have been written in 1971, the words have an ancient, timeless meaning. Jesus was born to live a sinless life, be crucified and die, to buy our pardon (forgiveness). He lives, and that is where our victory lies- in His resurrection!

***

The resurrection of Jesus is one of the most pivotal events in Christianity, fulfilling numerous prophecies from the Old Testament and confirming His divine identity as the Messiah. According to the Gospel accounts, Jesus was crucified, died, and was buried in a tomb. However, on the third day, He rose from the dead, conquering death and fulfilling God's plan of salvation. Jesus predicted His own resurrection multiple times in the scriptures to His disciples.

In **Matthew 16:21**, He tells them, *"From that time on Jesus began to explain to His disciples that He must go to Jerusalem and suffer many things... and that He must be killed and on the third day be raised to life."*

This declaration of rising on the third day became central to the Gospel message, demonstrating that His death was not the end but the beginning of God's plan to offer eternal life. The greatest gift God gave us is the gift of life and the gift of death.

In the beginning, Adam sinned and caused all mankind to be born into sin. They only way to get it back was by death. When Jesus was crucified on the cross, that was His plan to die, not Satan.

John 10:18 says, *"No one can take my life from me. I sacrifice it voluntarily. For I have the authority to lay it down when I want to and also to take it up again. For this is what my Father has commanded."*

The resurrection of Jesus also directly fulfilled Old Testament prophecies, specifically those that pointed to a suffering Messiah who would triumph over death. In **Psalm 16:10**, David wrote, *"Because you will not abandon me to the realm of the dead, nor will you let your faithful one see decay."* This prophecy is interpreted by the apostles as pointing to Jesus' resurrection. Peter refers to it in **Acts 2:31**, where he explains that David was speaking of the resurrection of Jesus, who did not see decay but rose on the third day.

Jesus' resurrection fulfilled this promise, showing that God's Holy One would not remain in the grave but would be raised to life, validating His divine nature and mission. Furthermore, the resurrection is crucial to the fulfillment of the Messianic prophecy found in **Isaiah 53:10-11**, which speaks of the suffering servant who would die for the sins of humanity. The passage describes how this servant, after suffering, would see the light of life and be satisfied.

Jesus' resurrection is the fulfillment of this promise, showing that after His atoning death, He would be vindicated by God and raised to new life, securing salvation for all who believe in Him.

In **Romans 4:25**, Paul writes, *"He was delivered over to death for our sins and was raised to life for our justification."* This highlights the connection between His death and resurrection as the basis for the justification of believers before God. The resurrection also validated Jesus' identity as the Son of God and the fulfillment of God's redemptive plan.

In **Matthew 28:6**, the angel at the tomb tells the women, *"He is not here; He has risen, just as He said."* This moment confirmed that Jesus was indeed who He claimed to be—the Son of God, the Messiah, the Savior of the world. The resurrection is the cornerstone of Christian faith, as Paul states in **1 Corinthians 15:17**, *"And if Christ has not been raised, your faith is futile; you are still in your sins."*

I used to be afraid of death. But not anymore.

The resurrection of Jesus was the greatest evidence that man's problem with sin was solved. If Jesus stayed in the tomb and had not risen, then the problem of sin would have not been solved. The resurrection of Jesus was the greatest promise of hope from the grave. If he had not come back from the grave, we would have no hope. The resurrection of Jesus was the greatest proof in history that death lost all power and authority over the earth. This is why Jesus had to die for all mankind which includes his journey to hell to release all those in captivity that died before him.

Matthew 27:50-52 says, *"Then Jesus shouted out again, and He released His spirit. At that moment the curtain in the sanctuary of the Temple was torn in two, from top to bottom. The earth shook, rocks split apart, and tombs opened. The bodies of many godly men and women who had died were raised from the dead."*

My Recollection Of Death

I remember staring at my dad in his casket and he had a very big smile on his face. When I last saw him in the hospital, he didn't have a smile, but at the funeral home, he did.

I asked the owner of the funeral home, "Did you do that to his face?"

She said "No, when I picked him up from the hospital, he had that smile on his face."

This showed me that death had no power over my dad. Death had to release him according to the scriptures because he lived in Christ which means he will never die. He is just sleeping.

1 Corinthians 15:22 says, "*Just as everyone dies because we all belong to Adam, everyone who belongs to Christ will be given new life.*"

Some people believe that Jesus Christ never rose from the dead. This was also told in the Bible after His resurrection. **Matthew 28:12-15** says, "*A meeting with the elders was called, and they decided to give the soldiers a large bribe. They told the soldiers, "You must say, 'Jesus' disciples came during the night while we were sleeping, and they stole his body.' If the governor hears about it, we'll stand up for you so you won't get in trouble." So, the guards accepted the bribe and said what they were told to say. Their story spread widely among the Jews, and they still tell it today.*"

This is the Bible. I cannot make this up. Go read it for yourself.

There are so many scriptures to show you that it was prophesied that He rose from the dead. Like the Bible said, still to this day, people are discussing the credibility of His resurrection and if it was real or not. However, people still cannot figure out who Jesus is.

But to everyone's amazement, He predicted everything before it happened. You know why? Because the Lord revealed these things to the kings and prophets in the Old Testament. That's right, remember all the stories that kings told, and prophets told, "God said, the Lord said."

When Jesus created the earth, He predicted his own death. **Genesis 3:15** describes how this would transpire, "*And I will put enmity between you and the woman, and between your offspring and hers; he will crush your head, and you will strike his heel.*"

Drumroll please…. It is not rocket science to see that Jesus was God. I will get to that later. Let's stick with the chapter at hand. He was a prophetic manifestation.

Here's what the Bible says about Jesus. Most of you have read the scripture before, if you read the Bible, **Isaiah 53:4-6** says, "*Yet it was our weaknesses He carried; it was our sorrows that weighed Him down. And we thought His troubles were a punishment from God, a punishment for His own sins! But He was pierced for our rebellion, crushed for our sins. He was beaten so we could be whole. He was whipped so we could be healed. All of us, like sheep, have strayed away. We have left God's paths to follow our own. Yet the Lord laid on Him the sins of us all.*"

Isaiah 53:7-9 says, "*He was oppressed and treated harshly, yet He never said a word. He was led like a lamb to the slaughter. And as a sheep is silent before the shearers, He did not open His mouth. Unjustly condemned, He was led away. No one cared that He died without descendants, that His life was cut short in midstream. But He was struck down for the rebellion of my people. He had done no wrong and had never deceived anyone. But He was buried like a criminal; He was put in a rich man's grave.*"

Wow, Jesus was desperately chasing our sins. But do you wonder if Isaiah prophesied about the resurrection? The scripture means even though He is dead, He will still rise to see his offspring.

Isaiah 53:11 reads, "*When He sees all that is accomplished by His anguish, He will be satisfied. And because of His experience, my righteous servant will make it possible for many to be counted righteous, for He will bear all their sins.*"

Jesus said over 2000 years ago, when He spoke to His disciples, that He received a command from His father, God. He said, *"He promised me if I lay my life down, I will still see the son that I bear. I will come back. I am convinced that if I die, I will be coming back."*

That's how we know that Jesus knew He was the Christ. It was that last statement; I will come back. You don't tell people that unless you know you're coming back. The fact that He repeated it over and over again, hundreds of years after Isaiah prophesied the same words.

Matthew 16:13-17 says, *"When Jesus came to the region of Caesarea Philippi, He asked His disciples, "Who do people say that the Son of Man is?" "Well," they replied, "Some say John the Baptist, some say Elijah, and others say Jeremiah or one of the other prophets." Then he asked them, "But who do **you** say I am?" Simon Peter answered, "You are the Messiah, the Son of the living God." Jesus replied, "You are blessed Simon, son of John, because my Father in heaven has revealed this to you. You did not learn this from any human being."*

There is that word ***Messiah***. All the prophets told people about the Messiah coming. Peter reveals it. WOW! Now that is a testimony within itself.

Matthew 16:21 says, *"From then on Jesus began to tell His disciples plainly that it was necessary for Him to go to Jerusalem, and that He would suffer many terrible things at the hands of the elders, the leading priests, and the teachers of religious law. He would be killed, but on the third day He would be raised from the dead."*

It's that part when He proves He was the Messiah. Anyone can say they're going to die and come back but really don't come back. You don't take chances dying, hoping you're coming back. The fact that He kept repeating it over and over again says He knew with a surety He would return.

They are going to kill me, but I'll be back. Not to mention, He timed it. He said, "In three days, I will be back."

The resurrection is confirmation of His Christ position. He was the Christ. Therefore, he was the greatest of all humans.

Matthew chapter **28:4-5**, says, *"The guards shook with fear when they saw him, and they fell into a dead faint. Then the angel spoke to the women. "Don't be afraid!" he said. "I know you are looking for Jesus, who was crucified. He isn't here! He is risen from the dead, just as He said would happen. Come, see where His body was lying."*

The angels said it exactly like He did. I am dropping the mic. Must I say more?

This is Jesus Christ, fulfilling the word of God that was prophesied about Him centuries prior. Through the resurrection, Jesus not only fulfilled the prophecies but also established the foundation for eternal life, offering hope to all who believe in His victory over sin and death.

I sincerely need you to understand the impact His resurrection has on your path to eternal life. He is the pattern and the one you should follow. This path is why Paul admonished us to follow him as he follows Christ… right to heaven.

Allow that to settle into your spirit because one day, you will follow the same path as Christ, and that pathway will lead you right to…. You guessed it: HEAVEN!!

Keep going, we have one more stop before you land at your destination.

Chapter 11

The Two Wars:
Light & Darkness

For the weapons of our warfare are not carnal, but mighty through God to the pulling down of strong holds.

-II Corinthians 10:14 (KJV)

We should recognize that light is inherently positive and reflects the nature, character, and presence of God. Before his rebellion, Satan was an angel of "light." However, **2 Corinthians 11:14** warns us that Satan and his demons can disguise themselves as angels of light, presenting a deceptive imitation. It is essential to discern between the true light that comes from God and the false light that only appears Godly. Satan seeks to deceive us into believing that his counterfeit light is pure and holy, when in reality, it is not.

The Bible describes two significant battles between God and Satan that symbolize the eternal struggle between light and darkness. The first war took place in heaven before the creation of the world.

In **Revelation 12:7-9**, it is written, *"Then war broke out in heaven: Michael and his angels fought against the dragon, and the dragon and his angels fought back. But he was not strong enough, and they lost their place in heaven. The great dragon was hurled down—that ancient serpent called the devil, or Satan, who leads the whole world astray."*

This cosmic conflict began when Satan, filled with pride, sought to exalt himself above God (**Isaiah 14:12-15**). However, the forces of light, led by God and His angels, triumphed over the darkness of Satan's rebellion. Satan and his followers were cast out of heaven, marking the first decisive victory of God's light over the forces of darkness.

The second war is prophesied to occur at the end of time, when Satan and his forces will gather for one final rebellion against God. **Revelation 20:7-10** describes how, after being released from his imprisonment, Satan will deceive the nations and lead them into battle against God. However, just as in the first war, darkness will once again be defeated by the overwhelming light of God's power. Fire will come down from heaven to consume Satan's armies, and he will be thrown into the lake of fire, where he will face eternal judgment. This final victory represents the ultimate triumph of light over darkness, as God's kingdom will be fully established, free from sin and evil forever.

These two wars serve as a testament to God's sovereignty and the certainty of His victory over all darkness. All the way to the end of the world, Jesus is going to fight for your spirit. He holds the key to life and death. If you are lost, He's coming to find you. Just like the parable of the lost sleep mentioned in **Matthew 18:12**.

Wow, this reminds me of my children. I will fight for them as long as I am living. I will never give up until I know they are doing well and free from trouble. That's how God feels about me and you.

The Path To Heaven

The path to heaven is one of the most profound spiritual journeys, and Jesus Christ provides the ultimate guide to navigating it. Through His life, teachings, and sacrifice, He offers a blueprint that leads to eternal life.

Jesus emphasizes that the way to heaven begins with faith in Him. In **John 14:6**, He declares, *"I am the way, the truth, and the life. No one comes to the Father except through me."* This statement underscores the necessity of trusting in Him as the Savior who bridges the gap between humanity and God. Through faith, believers are invited to enter a personal relationship with Christ, which becomes the foundation for their journey toward eternal life.

Jesus also teaches that repentance and obedience are critical components of the path to heaven. In **Matthew 4:17**, His first message is, *"Repent, for the kingdom of heaven has come near."* Repentance involves turning away from sin and seeking forgiveness from God. It is through this humility and genuine sorrow for wrongdoing that one's heart is transformed.

Jesus further calls His followers to live according to God's commandments, not merely as an obligation but as an act of love and devotion. Obedience reflects a changed heart, one that desires to align with God's will. Another essential aspect of Jesus' guidance is love—love for God and love for others.

When asked about the greatest commandment, Jesus replied in **Matthew 22:37-39**, *"'Love the Lord your God with all your heart and with all your soul and with all your mind.' This is the first and greatest commandment. And the second is like it: 'Love your neighbor as yourself.'"* This love is not passive but active, manifesting in acts of kindness, forgiveness, and service. By following His example of selfless love, believers demonstrate the character of Christ and fulfill God's desire for His people.

Jesus also emphasizes the importance of perseverance in faith. He warns in **Matthew 7:13-14** about the narrow gate and the difficult road that leads to life, highlighting that the journey is not without challenges. However, He promises His presence and strength to those who remain steadfast.

Through prayer, studying Scripture, and fellowship with other believers, individuals can draw closer to Jesus and find the courage to overcome obstacles. He provides assurance in **John 16:33**, *"In* *this world you will have trouble. But take heart! I have overcome the world."* This also offers hope and encouragement.

Ultimately, Jesus' death and resurrection provide the cornerstone of the way to heaven. Through His sacrifice, He pays the penalty for sin, making it possible for humanity to be reconciled with God. His resurrection affirms His victory over death and offers the promise of eternal life to all who believe.

By accepting Jesus as Lord and Savior, following His teachings, and living a life marked by faith, repentance, love, and perseverance, He shows us the way to inherit the eternal kingdom of heaven. Here are several Bible verses where Jesus speaks about entering the kingdom of heaven and eternal life:

John 14:6 says, *"I am the way, the truth, and the life. No one comes to the Father except through me."* Jesus emphasizes that He is the only path to the Father and, ultimately, to heaven.

Matthew 4:17 says, *"Repent, for the kingdom of heaven has come near."* Jesus begins His ministry by calling people to repentance as the first step toward entering the Kingdom.

Matthew 7:13-14 says, *"Enter through the narrow gate. For wide is the gate and broad is the road that leads to destruction, and many enter through it. But small is the gate and narrow the road that leads to life, and only a few find it."* Jesus teaches about the difficulty and commitment required to follow the path to eternal life.

John 3:3-5 says, *"Very truly I tell you, no one can see the kingdom of God unless they are born again."* Jesus explains to Nicodemus that spiritual rebirth through water and the Spirit is essential for entering God's kingdom.

Matthew 5:3 says, *"Blessed are the poor in spirit, for theirs is the kingdom of heaven."* These verses highlight the qualities of those who will inherit the Kingdom, such as being poor in spirit, merciful, and pure in heart.

Matthew 18:3 says, *"Truly I tell you, unless you change and become like little children, you will never enter the kingdom of heaven."* Jesus calls for humility and childlike faith to be part of His Kingdom.

Matthew 19:16-22 says, *"If you want to enter life, keep the commandments... If you want to be perfect, go, sell your possessions and give to the poor, and you will have treasure in heaven. Then come, follow me."* Jesus emphasizes obedience and self-sacrifice as part of following Him.

John 10:9 says, *"I am the gate; whoever enters through me will be saved. They will come in and go out and find pasture."* Jesus portrays Himself as the gateway to salvation and safety.

Luke 9:23-24 *"Whoever wants to be my disciple must deny themselves and take up their cross daily and follow me. For whoever wants to save their life will lose it, but whoever loses their life for me will save it."* Jesus speaks of the cost of discipleship as a pathway to eternal life.

John 11:25-26 says, *"I am the resurrection and the life. The one who believes in me will live, even though they die; and whoever lives by believing in me will never die. Do you believe this?"* Jesus promises eternal life to those who believe in Him.

These verses collectively highlight the importance of faith, repentance, humility, obedience, and surrendering to Christ as essential steps to entering the kingdom of heaven. Watch out. The devil is doing everything in his power to turn your back on God.

The War Of Darkness

Ready for the DARKNESS, here it is!

The Bible reveals several schemes and tactics employed by the devil to deceive, tempt, and lead people away from God. These schemes are designed to exploit human weaknesses and oppose God's plan.

Satan's primary tactic is to deceive. In **John 8:44**, Jesus describes him as *"a liar and the father of lies."* From the Garden of Eden, he deceived Eve by twisting God's word, saying, *"You will not certainly die"* (**Genesis 3:4**).

He continues to deceive humanity by making sin appear harmless or desirable. In **2 Corinthians 11:14**, Paul warns, *"Satan himself masquerades as an angel of light,"* showing how he can disguise evil as good. Satan often tempts people to satisfy their desires in ungodly ways.

In **Matthew 4:1-11**, he tempts Jesus in the wilderness, appealing to physical needs, pride, and power. This scheme is seen throughout scripture, as he lures people into sin through greed, lust, or other fleshly desires (**1 John 2:16**).

Another scripture in **Revelation 12:10** refers to Satan as *"the accuser of our brothers and sisters."* He accuses believers before God, as seen in the story of Job (**Job 1:9-11**). His goal is to sow guilt and shame, causing people to doubt God's forgiveness and love.

Satan works to create disunity among believers and within families. In **1 Corinthians 1:10-13**, Paul addresses divisions in the church, warning that such strife undermines God's work.

Ephesians 4:27 warns believers not to *"give the devil a foothold,"* indicating how unresolved anger and conflict can be exploited by him.

In **Genesis 3:1**, Satan begins his conversation with Eve by asking, *"Did God really say?"* This reveals his tactic of planting doubt about God's word and character. He continues this scheme by causing people to question God's promises, love, and justice. Satan often uses external pressures, such as persecution, to intimidate believers and weaken their faith.

In **1 Peter 5:8-9**, Peter warns, *"Your enemy the devil prowls around like a roaring lion looking for someone to devour."* Fear and intimidation are among his tools to silence or discourage God's people.

Satan introduces false teachings to lead people astray. In **1 Timothy 4:1**, Paul warns, *"The Spirit clearly says that in later times some will abandon the faith and follow deceiving spirits and things taught by demons."* By corrupting God's truth, he seeks to confuse and mislead. Pride was Satan's original downfall (**Isaiah 14:12-15**), and he uses it to ensnare others.

In **Proverbs 16:18**, it says, *"Pride goes before destruction."* He tempts people to rely on themselves rather than God, fostering arrogance and rebellion. Satan aims to discourage believers, making them feel defeated or unworthy.

In **2 Corinthians 4:8-9**, Paul acknowledges the pressures believers face but reminds them that God sustains them despite Satan's attempts to bring despair. Satan tries to block the progress of God's plans.

In **1 Thessalonians 2:18**, Paul says, *"For we wanted to come to you... but Satan blocked our way."* He works to create obstacles that hinder ministry and spiritual growth. Understanding these schemes helps believers stay vigilant.

Personal Deliverance

Galatians 5:1 says, *"Stand fast therefore in the liberty wherewith Christ hath made us free and be not entangled again with the yoke of bondage."*

It can be easy to be entangled with yokes of bondage and demons who invade your life because of sin or through your bloodline. Without going in too deeply with this subject (as many have already written on it), I want to give you some basic keys to work through your deliverance and cast out your own demons. This is a vital part of your salvation and must be ongoing, not one occurrence.

Deliverance is offering up from your life anything that does not look like or resemble God. When you deliver yourself from sin and sinful behaviors, then you should work daily to ensure your soul is healed and your spirit remains pure and in its holiest form.

To make this plainer, here are a few root spirits that you may need to seek 'deliverance' from:

- Infirmity
- Perversion
- Pride
- Rejection
- Torment
- Haughtiness
- Abandonment
- Jealousy

These are just a few to help you identify what may need to be cast out. As you identify what needs to be purged from your life, I want you to take time daily to pray about your deliverance and do the work it takes to be free. Seek additional resources, prayer books and audios to help you maintain your freedom.

Remember, **Matthew 12:43-45** tells us what happens when we do not fill the space in our lives where demons have been cast out. It says, "*When the unclean spirit is gone out of a man, he walketh through dry places, seeking rest, and findeth none. Then he saith, I will return into my house from whence I came out; and when he is come, he findeth it empty, swept, and garnished. Then goeth he, and taketh with himself seven other spirits more wicked than himself, and they enter in and dwell there: and the last state of that man is* *worse than the first. Even so shall it be also unto this wicked generation."*

This scripture warns us of the danger of not filling ourselves with the word of God (the Bible), or the Holy Spirit. When we remain empty, we leave ourselves open to spiritual attacks that can lead to more spiritual death. I have written a prayer for you to pray to cast the demons out of your life, perform self-deliverance and fill your temple with the Holy Spirit.

In your prayer time, pray this prayer and fill in the blanks with the name of the spirit that you are casting out:

In the mighty name of Jesus, I come against the spirit of _____ and I bind your activities in my life!

In the name of Jesus, I take full authority over the spirit of _____ and I lose myself from your grip!

I cancel your legal right in my life, and I command you to be gone in the name of Jesus! Be removed from my life! You cannot and will not enter my temple anymore! I declare that the spirit of the Lord washed and redeemed me by the blood of the Lamb, and I have been set free!

I fill my temple with your Holy Spirit and Father, I ask that every void be filled, giving no room or place to the enemy. I am a vessel who is sanctified and filled with the Spirit of the Living God, and nothing shall by any means hurt me!

Thank you, Jesus, for setting me free so that I walk in victory daily. In Jesus name I pray, amen!

The Whole Armor Of God

The work of deliverance does not begin and end with casting out the demons who torment you. It continues with putting on the full armor of God, so you can withstand the wiles of the wicked one.

Ephesians 6:11 advises to *"Put on the full armor of God, so that you can take your stand against the devil's schemes."* By relying on God's truth and strength, believers can resist his tactics. All in all, which side will you choose?

To effectively win the war against darkness, I will end this chapter by admonishing you to put on your full armor. Once you put the armor on, there will be times you will need to fortify your armor or enforce it when experiencing times of intense warfare. I will introduce you to the parts of the spiritual armor, then we will end with a prayer for you to pray to assist you in putting it on.

Take time to memorize the parts of the spiritual armor if you are not already familiar with them.

Now pray this prayer to put on and reinforce your armor when times of warfare become intense:

Heavenly Father,

I come before You in humility and faith, acknowledging that the battle I face is not against flesh and blood but against spiritual forces of evil in the heavenly realms.

ARMOR OF GOD — Helmet Of Salvation — Praying In The Spirit — Breastplate Of Righteousness — Belt Of Truth — SHIELD OF FAITH — Sword Of The Spirit — Shoes Of Peace

I thank You for equipping me with Your divine armor to stand firm and victorious. Today, I put on the whole armor of God as You

command in Ephesians 6:10-20, trusting in Your strength to sustain me.

Lord, I gird my waist with the belt of truth.

Let Your truth hold me steady, grounding me in Your Word and protecting me from the deception of the enemy. Help me to walk in honesty, integrity, and unwavering trust in Your promises.

I put on the breastplate of righteousness.

Guard my heart, Lord, with Your righteousness. Help me to live in a way that reflects Your holiness, shielding me from sin and the accusations of the enemy. I thank You for the righteousness that comes through faith in Christ.

I shod my feet with the preparation of the gospel of peace.

Lord, guide my steps to share Your message of hope and reconciliation. Let me walk boldly and confidently, bringing peace wherever I go, as an ambassador of Your kingdom.

I take up the shield of faith.

Strengthen my faith, Father, to extinguish every fiery dart of doubt, fear, and temptation the enemy sends my way. I trust in Your power to protect me and in Your promises to sustain me.

I put on the helmet of salvation.

Guard my mind with the assurance of my salvation. Help me to think on things that are true, noble, and pure, so I may not be shaken by the lies of the enemy. Let the hope of eternal life anchor me in every trial.

I take up the sword of the Spirit, which is Your Word.

Lord, fill my heart and mouth with Your Word, which is alive and powerful. Teach me to wield it wisely and effectively, cutting through every lie and standing firm in the truth.

I commit to praying in the Spirit on all occasions.

Holy Spirit, guide me in prayer. Align my heart with the Father's will, and intercede through me with groanings too deep for words. Let my prayers be persistent and fervent for myself, for my brothers and sisters in Christ, and for the advancement of Your kingdom.

Lord, I pray for boldness as an ambassador in bonds.

Even in chains or challenges, may I proclaim the mystery of the Gospel fearlessly, just as Paul did. Strengthen me to be Your representative, wherever I am, and to share the Good News without compromise or hesitation.

Father, I know that the battle belongs to You, and in You, I am more than a conqueror. As I go forth today, clothed in Your armor, help me to stand firm, resist the enemy, and remain steadfast in faith. May everything I do bring glory to Your name and extend the victory of Christ on this Earth.

In the mighty name of Jesus, I pray, Amen.

***

The battle between God's light and Satan's darkness is not just a cosmic conflict but a reality that touches every heart, home, and nation. It is the struggle between truth and deception, holiness and sin, life and death. Yet, throughout Scripture, we see the unshakable truth: God's light is victorious. *"The light shines in the darkness, and the darkness has not overcome it"* (**John 1:5**).

This war is a call to vigilance for every believer, reminding us to stand firm in the armor of God, equipped with faith, truth, and the Word of God. While the enemy seeks to blind and destroy, we are called to walk as children of light, reflecting God's love, truth, and holiness in a darkened world.

Ultimately, the war has already been won through Jesus Christ. His death and resurrection have disarmed the powers of darkness and secured eternal victory for all who follow Him (**Colossians 2:15**).

As His followers, we do not fight for victory—we fight from victory. Our role is to live boldly as ambassadors of His light, resisting the schemes of the enemy and proclaiming the Gospel until the day He returns to banish darkness forever.

Let us remember that the power of God's light is greater than any force of darkness. By remaining steadfast in His truth, empowered by His Spirit, and grounded in His Word, we can stand firm amid this spiritual battle, knowing that the kingdom of light will prevail. *"For the Lord will be your everlasting light, and your God will be your glory"* (**Isaiah 60:19**).

Now, whose side will you be on? What side do you choose? As you can see, the Israelites in the desert had to learn the hard way, but you got it easy. Jesus came and died for you, so now choose!

Chapter 12

Your Salvation Is Sealed. You Made It To Heaven!

In him we have redemption through his blood, the forgiveness of sins, in accordance with the riches of God's grace.

-Ephesians 1:7

Receiving salvation is the cornerstone of the Christian faith, as it represents the gift of eternal life and reconciliation with God. Salvation is rooted in the grace of God and is freely offered to all who believe in Jesus Christ.

Ephesians 2:8-9 explains, *"For it is by grace you have been saved, through faith—and this is not from yourselves, it is the gift of God—not by works, so that no one can boast."*

This passage highlights that salvation is not earned by human efforts but is a divine gift, accessible through faith in Jesus Christ as Lord and Savior. The pathway to salvation begins with repentance, a heartfelt acknowledgment of sin and turning toward God.

Acts 3:19 states, *"Repent, then, and turn to God, so that your sins may be wiped out, that times of refreshing may come from the Lord."*

Repentance involves recognizing one's need for forgiveness and desiring a new life in Christ. This step is essential because it opens the heart to receive God's mercy and the transforming power of His Spirit. Repentance is not just sorrow for sin but a decision to change direction and follow God's will. Faith in Jesus Christ is central to receiving salvation.

In **John 3:16**, one of the most well-known verses in the Bible, Jesus declares, *"For God so loved the world that he gave his one and only*

Son, that whoever believes in him shall not perish but have eternal life." Believing in Jesus means trusting in His death and resurrection as the only means of forgiveness and reconciliation with God.

Romans 10:9 further emphasizes, *"If you declare with your mouth, 'Jesus is Lord,' and believe in your heart that God raised Him from the dead, you will be saved."* Faith is not just an intellectual assent but a personal trust that transforms the heart and life. Baptism is another important step that symbolizes salvation and the believer's new identity in Christ.

In **Acts 2:38**, Peter tells the crowd, *"Repent and be baptized, every one of you, in the name of Jesus Christ for the forgiveness of your sins. And you will receive the gift of the Holy Spirit."* Baptism is an outward expression of an inward transformation, signifying the washing away of sins and the Believer's commitment to live for Christ.

While baptism itself does not save, it serves as a public declaration of faith and obedience to God's command. Salvation culminates in a life lived in fellowship with God, marked by obedience and ongoing transformation.

2 Corinthians 5:17 states, *"Therefore, if anyone is in Christ, the new creation has come: The old has gone, the new is here!"* Those who receive salvation are empowered by the Holy Spirit to live a new life that reflects God's love, grace, and truth.

Salvation is not only about escaping eternal judgment but also about experiencing abundant life in Christ here and now (**John 10:10**). Through faith, repentance, baptism, and a life of devotion, believers enter a relationship with God that brings eternal hope and joy.

Paul's writings in the Bible contain profound teachings on receiving eternal life. He emphasizes that it is a gift from God, obtained through faith in Jesus Christ rather than human effort.

In **Romans 6:23,** Paul writes, *"For the wages of sin is death, but the gift of God is eternal life in Christ Jesus our Lord."* This verse highlights the contrast between the consequences of sin—spiritual death—and the unearned gift of eternal life provided through Christ's sacrifice. Paul underscores that eternal life is a free gift from God, rooted in His grace. Paul also emphasizes the role of faith in Jesus Christ as the pathway to eternal life.

In Ephesians **2:8-9,** he states, *"For it is by grace you have been saved, through faith— and this is not from yourselves, it is the gift of God—not by works, so that no one can boast."* Faith is the key to salvation and eternal life, and it is through belief in the death and resurrection of Jesus that one is justified and made righteous before God.

Paul reiterates this in **Romans 10:9,** saying, *"If you declare with your mouth, 'Jesus is Lord,' and believe in your heart that God raised him from the dead, you will be saved."* In addition to faith, Paul speaks about living a life guided by the Spirit as evidence of one's eternal inheritance.

In **Galatians 6:8,** he writes, *"Whoever sows to please their flesh, from the flesh will reap destruction; whoever sows to please the Spirit, from the Spirit will reap eternal life."* This highlights the transformative power of the Holy Spirit in the believer's life, guiding them away from sin and toward righteousness as they await the fullness of eternal life.

Paul also connects eternal life with perseverance in doing good and seeking God's glory. In **Romans 2:6-7,** he explains, *"God 'will* *repay each person according to what they have done.' To those who by persistence in doing good seek glory, honor, and immortality, he will give eternal life."* This passage shows that eternal life is not just a future promise but is also reflected in a life dedicated to God's purposes, driven by faith and obedience.

Finally, Paul reminds believers that eternal life is secured through the resurrection of Jesus Christ. In **1 Corinthians 15:54-57**, he proclaims, *"Death has been swallowed up in victory... Thanks be to God! He gives us the victory through our Lord Jesus Christ."* Paul assures that through Christ's triumph over death, believers have the hope of eternal life.

For Paul, eternal life is both a present reality and a future promise, given to all who put their trust in Christ and live by the Spirit. Here's the good news that you need to remember and if you confess with your mouth and believe in your heart until the end of the world, then I'll see you in Heaven!

The Certainty Of Salvation

The glorious truth of salvation is that it is a work of God, sealed by His Spirit, and guaranteed for all who place their faith in Jesus Christ. As Believers, we can have absolute confidence that our salvation is secure, not because of our efforts but because of God's unchanging promises. The seal of the Holy Spirit is the mark of our eternal inheritance, ensuring that we are forever His (**Ephesians 1:13-14**).

When you stand in the presence of God in heaven, it will not be because of your good works, achievements, or strength, but because of Jesus' sacrifice on the cross and your faith in Him. You will hear the words every believer longs to hear: *"Well done, good and faithful servant. Enter into the joy of your Lord"* (**Matthew 25:23**). Heaven is not just a destination; it is the fulfillment of God's ultimate promise, where we will dwell with Him in perfect love, peace, and joy forever.

Let this assurance strengthen your faith, embolden your witness, and deepen your gratitude. Salvation is sealed, heaven is real, and through Christ, the victory is eternally yours.

The Confidence Of Your Eternal Life

Salvation is the greatest gift God has given to humanity—a gift that ensures not only forgiveness of sins but also eternal life in His presence. This journey through the truths of Scripture has revealed the depth of God's love, the sufficiency of Christ's sacrifice, and the assurance of our heavenly inheritance.

From understanding who God is, to embracing the life, death, and resurrection of Jesus, to exploring the covenants, commandments, and the work of the Spirit, this book has sought to answer the critical question: Can salvation get you into heaven? The answer is resoundingly YES! Salvation is not about what we do but about what Christ has already done.

As you close this book, let your heart rest in the knowledge that your salvation is secure. Walk boldly in your faith, knowing that God has prepared a place for you in heaven. Live in the light of this truth, sharing the good news with others, and looking forward to the day when you will see your Savior face-to-face.

"And this is the testimony: God has given us eternal life, and this life is in His Son. Whoever has the Son has life; whoever does not have the Son of God does not have life" (**1 John 5:11-12**).

May you walk in the confidence of your salvation, the joy of your relationship with Christ, and the hope of eternal life in heaven. To God be the glory forever and ever.

HELP ME SPREAD THE GOOD NEWS THAT GOD BECAME MAN IN JESUS CHRIST. HE LIVED THE LIFE WE SHOULD HAVE LIVED, AND DIED THE DEATH WE SHOULD HAVE DIED... IN OUR PLACE.

THREE DAYS LATER, HE ROSE FROM THE DEAD, PROVING THAT HE IS THE SON OF GOD, AND OFFERING THE GIFT OF SALVATION AND FORGIVENESS OF SINS TO ANYONE WHO REPENTS AND BELIEVES IN HIM.

AMEN, AMEN, AMEN!!!

If you have never accepted Jesus Christ into your heart, take some time to pray this prayer, wherever you are. When you pray this prayer of repentance, know that your fate is sealed… you are going to heaven!

Prayer of Repentance & Salvation

Heavenly Father,

I come to You today, recognizing my need for Your grace and forgiveness. I acknowledge that I am a sinner, and I have fallen short of Your glory. I have lived my life according to my own desires, and I confess my sins before You now.

Lord, I repent of my sins. I turn away from everything that separates me from You and ask for Your forgiveness. Cleanse my heart and make me new. I believe that Jesus Christ is Your Son, that He died on the cross for my sins, and that He rose from the dead to give me eternal life.

Today, I surrender my life to You, and I accept Jesus Christ as my Lord and Savior. I place my faith in Him alone for my salvation. Lead me by Your Holy Spirit and help me to follow You all the days of my life. Strengthen me to live according to Your Word and to walk in the light of Your truth.

Thank You for Your love, Your mercy, and the gift of salvation. I rejoice that I am now a child of God, sealed by Your Spirit, and have the promise of eternal life with You.

In Jesus' name, I pray,
Amen.

ABOUT THE AUTHOR

Patricia Tanner was born and raised in Sanford FL. She comes from a family of three siblings. Patricia Tanner is the founder of Multhai International Realty, Multhai Asset Management Services, and Multhai Investment Group which is in Sanford, Florida. She is a graduate of the University of Central Florida, where she received a Bachelor of Science in Business Administration and a minor in Human Resources Management.

Patricia began her career shortly thereafter as a Regional Property Manager in the apartment community. Throughout her career in property management, she has built interpersonal relationships with corporate clients. She has a successful track record of increasing company revenues over $5 million annually, through hard work, commitment, creativeness, and strategic planning.

Her experience and leadership role eventually led her to achieve a Florida Real Estate Broker license. She spent fifteen years in the Real Estate field while completing a Master of Arts in Human Resources Management from Webster University, and a Master of Public Administration from Troy University. It was in this capacity that she decided to open her own brokerage company, Multhai International Realty.

In addition, Patricia finds time in her busy to participate in her own Non For Profit Organization, Stones 2 Homes. She remains President of her organization in which she helps people build, keep, or purchase homes in affordable communities. She is the founder of PNT Property Partners in which she buys vacant land, develops them, and constructs brand new construction homes in Sanford Florida. Her overall goal is to educate and provide resources to help people overcome financial hardships and credit disadvantage to live the American Dream through homeownership in spite of economic hardship. Through her visions she will continue to grow as an entrepreneur and is willing to share her knowledge, experience, and expertise with anyone whom is willing to learn.

MORE BOOKS BY THE AUTHOR

30 Days Of Grieving

Given By The Inspiration Of God

Healing From COVID-19

Almost a year later, and it hit me... My mother was gone, and I was still stuck at the hospital. I had tried everything from crying to counseling, and even prayer. Pray they told me. Trust God they insisted. But it seemed as if nothing was working. I was hurt, dealing with my reality: my mother was not coming back.

While journeying through grief, it was under the divine 'Inspiration of God' that He placed me in a trance. While I was gaining a revelation about grief, He gave me this journal, '30 Days Of Grieving.'

NOW AVAILABLE:
WWW.Amazon.Com

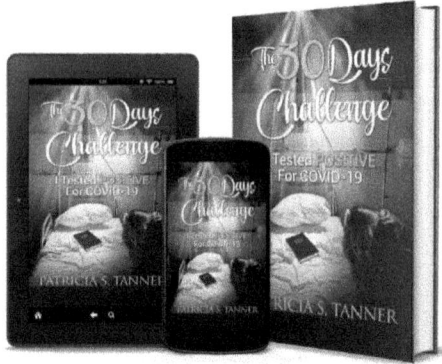

The 30 Days Challenge:
I Tested POSITIVE for COVID-19

If you had 30 days to live, what would you do? If you were told that you needed to prepare for a marathon in 30 days and you were completely out of shape, what would you do first? If a family member handed you one million dollars and told you that you had to figure out how to build a house (debt free), how would you execute your plan?

I'm catching you off guard with these requests, right? Well, this is exactly what COVID-19 did when it snatched my mother's life away, wrecking my entire world. I had to battle for my mother AND my faith in 30 days flat. What a challenge!

Throughout this book, I will walk you through my brief journey with COVID-19, negative of a happy ending. I will share the diary I kept while attending to my mother, and the scriptures I read, prayed, and quoted as my shield and protection.

Take the journey with me, there is healing on the other side!

NOW AVAILABLE:
WWW.Amazon.Com

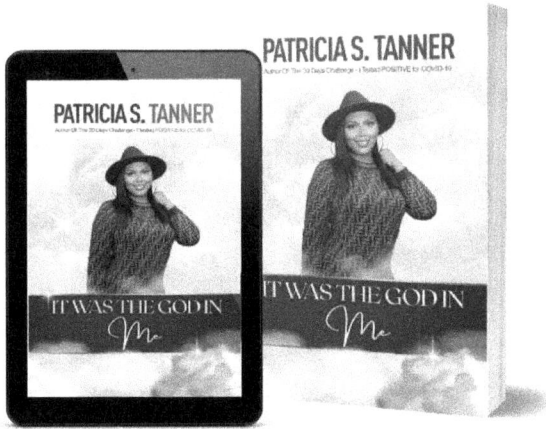

It Was The God In

Me

Success can be attributed to many things. Depending on the person who has obtained success would determine those to whom they attribute their success. Some give credit to their daily routine while others give credit to a mentor or some sort of system they followed. When I think about my success, the only person who I can give the credit to is God.

In this memoir, I share the successes and failures I have experienced throughout my life. From my individual experiences to my entrepreneurial journey, I share how God has walked with me every step of the way.

Come and see.. It Was The God In Me!!

NOW AVAILABLE:
WWW.Amazon.Com

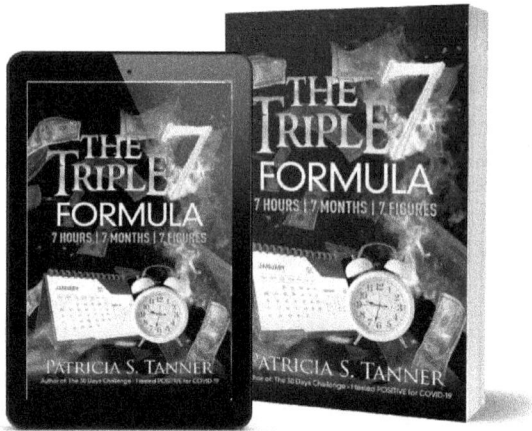

The Triple 7 Formula is designed for business owners who are looking forward to hitting the million-dollar mark in their business. If you own a business and seem to be running in financial circles, this book will get you on track to simultaneously gaining sound business structure and millions in your bank account.

It was through many conversations with business owners in lack of financial gain that prompted Patricia to share her blueprint for millionaire status. Through this book, she demonstrates how to gain financial ground by developing strong teams, implementing systems, and setting stackable goals. If you are ready to gain a laser sharp focus, and implement these clear steps, you will position yourself for financial greatness. Your business will be sound, and you will see financial growth beyond your wildest dreams!!

NOW AVAILABLE:
WWW.Amazon.Com

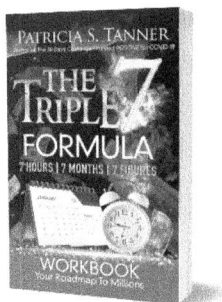

The Triple 7 Formula is specifically crafted for business owners aspiring to reach the million-dollar milestone. If you are a business owner feeling stuck in financial cycles, this book will set you on the path to building both a solid business structure and financial success.

This workbook is designed to complement the textbook of the same name. As you progress through its pages, you will be inspired to take decisive steps toward becoming a millionaire. From constructing your business framework to creating the millionaire's avatar, this process will expand your knowledge and mindset. Not only will you chart a course to financial success, but you will also identify your accountability circle and select a mentor to guide you toward greatness.

I cannot guarantee millionaire status unless you actively follow the steps to begin your journey. If you are searching for a get rich quick scheme, this workbook is not for you. I am looking for those ready to put in the effort—and since you are reading this, I believe that's you!

You have finally found it: Your roadmap to millions!

NOW AVAILABLE:
WWW.Amazon.Com

PATRICIA S. TANNER

Find Patricia on The Web:

https://PatriciaTanner.com

Follow Patricia on social media:

Facebook & Instagram: @PatriciaTannerInc

PATRICIA S. TANNER

www.ingramcontent.com/pod-product-compliance
Lightning Source LLC
Chambersburg PA
CBHW060356090426
42734CB00011B/2148